PREACHING THROUGH HOLY DAYS AND HOLIDAYS

SERMONS
THAT WORK
XI

Editors

Roger Alling is president of the Episcopal Preaching Foundation, and director of the Foundation's highly regarded Preaching Excellence Program for students in Episcopal Seminaries. He has edited each volume in the *Sermons that Work* series. He has been a parish priest and diocesan stewardship officer, and currently serves as priest associate in southwest Florida. On behalf of the Foundation he presents diocesan conferences on preaching.

David J. Schlafer is a former philosophy professor and seminary sub-dean who has taught homiletics at a number of seminaries in several denominations and at the College of Preachers. Author or editor of ten books on preaching, he is an individual consultant and conference leader throughout the United States and England.

Edited by

Roger Alling *and* David J. Schlafer

Morehouse Publishing

NEW YORK • HARRISBURG • DENVER

Unless otherwise noted, the Scripture quotations contained herein are from the New Revised Standard Version Bible, copyright © 1989 by the Division of Christian Education of the National Council of Churches of Christ in the U.S.A. Used by permission. All rights reserved.

Morehouse Publishing, 4775 Linglestown Road, Harrisburg, PA 17112

Morehouse Publishing, 445 Fifth Avenue, New York, NY 10016

Morehouse Publishing is an imprint of Church Publishing Incorporated.
www.churchpublishing.org

Library of Congress Cataloging-in-Publication Data

     Preaching through holy days and holidays / edited by Roger Alling and
David J. Schlafer.
        p. cm.—(Sermons that work ; 11)
     Includes bibliographical references.
     ISBN 978-0-8192-1892-6 (pbk.)
     1. Episcopal Church—Sermons. 2. Sermons, American. 3. Church year
sermons. 4. Episcopal preaching (Episcopal Church) I. Alling, Roger,
1933- II. Schlafer, David J., 1944- III. Series.
BX5937.A1 P7455 2003
252'.6—dc21

2002010473

Printed in the United States of America

CONTENTS

3 Feasts of the Saints

4 Celebrations of Ministerial Vocation

5 Civil Holidays

INTRODUCTION

Speaking Grace through Special Occasions

"*What's new?*" This common, casual greeting says something significant: sooner or later, "business as usual" gets boring. "Variety is the spice of life," the old adage runs. Routines, professional and domestic, are more cheerfully managed if the ordinary is graced, now and then, with something fresh—something unusual.

So it is with sermons. Preachers are charged with telling and retelling "the old, old story." (They may, in fact, be chargeable with heresy if they *don't.*) In company with St. Paul, the Church proclaims Jesus Christ "the same, yesterday, today, and forever." But if it always does so in the same old way, nobody listens very well—or very long. A bishop of recent memory had a reputation for preaching the identical sermon at every confirmation service on his round of parish visitations. Questioned about his homiletical monotony, he cheerfully responded: "When people do what I've said in *that* sermon, I'll preach *another* one!" His answer evoked half-hearted chuckles—and internal winces.

The challenge, then: how can preachers cultivate *appropriate* expressions of sermon variety—*not* substitutes for theological substance, superficial sprinkles of novelty over otherwise indistinguishable bowls of weekly sermon porridge?

To that important question there is no single answer. Careful students of Scripture, surely, are never at a loss for fresh resources. Those who love God, love people, and love words continually refine the forms of their preaching artistry. Constantly changing social issues and the continuing fresh heart cries of those in congregations—all these offer inexhaustible wellsprings of imagination and insight. There are *no instant recipes*, yet there are abundant *fruitful resources* for healthy variety in preaching.

But *why*—it merits asking—why does "Preacher, what's new?" play persistently in the minds of sermon listeners (even if that question is not verbalized)? Long ago, on a hill in Athens, St. Paul encountered a jaded audience of philosophers who were interested "in nothing but telling or hearing something new." Does today's preacher occupy a similar space? Is the desire for "something different" on the part of sermon listeners simply a demand for the "new and improved," coming from overstimulated consumers in a multi-media culture?

No. Definitely not. "What's new, Preacher?" is, at heart, an inarticulate hunger for theological orientation and direction. The question expresses a yearning for preaching that offers a faith perspective-in-process. People need an unfolding, intelligible frame of faith reference—an interpreting lens for lives they experience as vaguely patterned at best, utterly chaotic at worst. A longing for new insight, fresh perspective on life's journeying is always *implicit* in those who come to church.

On so-called "special occasions," however, that deep desire for clarifying direction surges irrepressibly to the *surface*. High Times—specific celebrations of joy, grief, gratitude, loss, vocation, transition, remembrance, and renewal in the life of a community—all these call out, insistently and rightly, for a timely word from the preacher of the day. Sermons well preached on such occasions often make life-changing differences for individuals and communities. Sermons poorly presented on special occasions do far more lasting harm than "ordinary" sermons. And for good reason.

The "special day" itself has the significance it does because of what those present have "been through," what has "brought them here." The day has "moment" because of where, in light of the moment, those who have convened for the special occasion will "go from here." On a special occasion, time pauses, stands still. Listeners wait for a word of direction, fitly spoken, that will make a difference.

Such a word will not come if the preacher skirts the occasion, talking "around" it. A word that simply dispenses information "about" the "issues raised by this day" will, in all probability, leave listeners unengaged (maybe even stuck). A presumptuous prophetic word—spoken not just "to" but "at" us—telling us what "we now must do," because of what this day "really means," will *not* effectively empower us.

What we need is a word that guides us, *through* this occasion, toward God's inviting call. A special occasion is a day on which we do not want simply to mark time—but, rather, to MARK TIME. All times are in God's hands. We may assent to, even strongly believe, that abstract theological fact. Nevertheless, we have a need, perhaps an *urgent* need, to know how, specifically, God holds our time on *this* day.

Some of these days are ones that we know are coming—holy days and holidays of different sorts and different levels of magnitude—Christmas, Easter, Mothers' Day, Memorial Day. What makes other days special—sometimes terrifyingly so—is the sudden in-breaking of the utterly unexpected—the fall of the Berlin Wall, the fall of the World Trade Towers. The spectrum of "occasional service preaching" is as wide as the world. Just as there is no simple recipe for sermon variety, generally, so there is no one-size-fits-all formula to which preachers can automatically resort in preparing for sermons on special occasions.

But the underlying question on such days is always the same, for listener and preacher alike: This day *is* different! Is there a Word from the Lord that will *make* a difference? If, as Scripture says, God is "making all things new," then *where—how—here—now*—on this particular, unusual day?[1]

The sermons in this volume are attempts by a "great company of preachers" to engage that question with integrity and imagination. The authors are as diverse as the occasions they address. The attempt, however, in every preaching event, is to hold up for celebration the distinctive aspect of Amazing Grace particularly evident on that occasion. Each sermon affirms a universal, unconditional grace taking tangible form in a particular time, place, and condition. As such, for all their particularity, immediacy, and non-transferability, these sermons also offer an insight into the preaching enterprise entire. What makes *these* sermons work? The same thing, ultimately, that makes *any* sermon work—the sanctifying, through words, of particular places and times, by gesturing toward incarnations evident therein of all-surrounding, all-suffusing Love.

Those familiar with *Sermons that Work* will recognize two recurring features in the last three sections of this volume: sermons and addresses from the annual Preaching Excellence Conference sponsored by the Foundation that produces this anthology series, and invited essays of special interest to preachers by distinguished guest authors. The rich and provocative essays by A. Katherine Grieb on preaching from Pauline epistles and by Richard Ward and Joanne Buchanan-Brown on preaching as a performance art are not specifically concerned with "special occasion" preaching. As you will shortly discover, however, they are (like the conference sermons that follow them) very much in resonance with the tenor and tone of this volume.

Once more, the editors express their profound appreciation to Morehouse Publishing for making this series available to an increasingly wider and more enthusiastic audience.

---

1. Special occasion preaching as a critical area for homiletical attention is explored systematically in *What Makes This Day Different? Preaching Grace on Special Occasions*, by David J. Schlafer. (Cambridge, Mass.: Cowley Publications, 1998).

CHRISTMAS EVE

Christmas Trees

Luke 2:1-20
Emily J. Schnabl

IF YOU HAD ASKED me last week what comes to mind when I think of Christmas trees, three images would have popped into my head. The first would be putting up the family Christmas tree. Dragged by my father down slippery Chicago sidewalks to our apartment, then set up by the three of us—all having strong (and different) opinions about which way it was leaning, which was its best side—all of us sticky and scratched by the time it was finally in place. With its treasured ornaments and rituals, that annual tree reminds me of shared family moments.

Then there is the fantasy tree—the one children got to eat breakfast under in Marshall Field's Walnut Room. It stretched for eight floors in the department store courtyard. You could gaze at the top while waiting for Santa. That tree reminds me of winter holiday enchantment.

Being Gen X, one of my trees is the Charlie Brown Christmas tree, its funny bare branches reminding me of the least likely, the littlest, the underdog, coming out on top at the most important moment.

But on Friday evening's news I saw another tree I have not been able to get out of my mind. Did you see it? It wasn't a tall tree. It wasn't even real. There were no presents underneath. Instead of gracing a living room bay window, it was set among the rubble of the destroyed home of a Palestinian Christian family in Bethlehem. Its ornaments were not family heirlooms or expensive creations—they were spent rifle casings the family found among the ruins of their home.

Aesthetically it was uglier even than Charlie Brown's tree. But, standing in a ruined house in the little town of Bethlehem, in danger of being toppled by yet another tank or bullet, that tree speaks more to me about the Christmas story than any other tree I've ever seen.

We tend to forget, I think, about how fragile and dangerous was Christ's coming into our world. How tenuous was Mary's life once it was discovered she was unmarried and pregnant—public shame being the least of her worries. Childbirth in those days was risky even for wealthy women, let alone for a young woman of uncertain means traveling in her ninth month of pregnancy from Nazareth to Bethlehem. The registration toward which Joseph was heading was part of an oppressive tax system administered by corrupt officials.

God chose an unstable time, an unsettled place. Just as our Palestinian sisters and brothers did not wait to restore their house to perfect order before they put up their Christmas tree, God did not wait for us to get it right before coming into the world. The Palestinian family took what was around them—plastic, metal, concrete—and put up a sign of hope. God took what was around—a small country, a poor woman with an amazingly understanding husband, a stable next to an inn, and gave us a baby to be our sign of hope. God didn't wait for us to get our house in order. God came anyway.

As the angels said, that is good news of great joy. It is such good news that generations of turning Christmas into a spending, partying rush has not diluted its power. If there were not such power and truth at the heart of Christmas, it would not have survived. Holidays come and go—we don't celebrate too many Roman or medieval feast days, after all—but the fact that God enters the rubble of our lives as a vulnerable infant cannot be overcome by free holiday shipping and three months of Christmas Muzak. The fact that God comes down as a baby, asking humans to hold him, feed him, and treasure him, cannot be overcome by rushing around, trying to put together the perfect Christmas.

God took a poor young woman and asked her to be the mother of God. God used a stable full of animals and made it the birthplace of the Prince of Peace. God took rough shepherds and made them the messengers of good news. Bullets become ornaments on a Christmas tree; our weaknesses and sins become the glory of God.

The lights of Christmas enchant and delight, but they also reveal the cracks in our lives we work so hard to paper over. That Bethlehem Christmas tree didn't paper over the cracks, didn't hide the truth. It told the truth. Soreness of heart is real. And Christ's coming doesn't fix that soreness in ways we want it to. When we fix the world the way we want it to, eventually it goes wrong, and we destroy even more in the process. No, God says, let's do it my way, with my own life and death and new life.

The childhood visions of Christmas are still real. Christmas is about the rituals we share as families. Christmas is about fantasy and delight.

Christmas is about the underdog getting the best present under the tree. But even those wonderful things are shadows of God's love for us, a love that finds its way in through cracks and rubble. On this Christmas, we open ourselves to beholding signs of hope that the dear Christ has entered in, two thousand years ago in Bethlehem, in Bethlehem today, in our hearts here and now.

Emily J. Schnabl is Curate of St. George's Church,
Belleville, Illinois.

ASH WEDNESDAY

What a Paradox Faith Is!

Joel 2:1-2, 12-17; Matthew 6:1-6, 16-21
Mary Frances Schjonberg

WHAT A PARADOX this night is! In a few moments, I will invite you forward to smear ashes on your forehead—perhaps the most visibly enduring of Christian rituals. There is no physical evidence on Sunday afternoon that we have received communion in the morning. You can't tell just by looking if someone has been baptized or confirmed. But the smudge of ashes, the sign of the cross on your forehead—*that* is visible to everyone.

I will admit that I went to the bank this morning before the noon service, just so I wouldn't have to walk around with these ashes on my forehead. But God sometimes is a trickster. I forgot I had a chiropractor appointment this afternoon. So there I went with my ashes. To my relief, when I walked in, I saw that the chiropractor and people in the waiting room had ashes too.

Why, then, does Jesus tell us to "beware of practicing your piety before others in order to be seen by them"? Some in Jesus' time made a show of their prayers, hoping to impress onlookers and, perhaps, God. Why does Joel, an early practitioner of the sound bite, put it more succinctly still? "Rend your heart and not your clothing"? In his day, people demonstrated repentance for sin by tearing their clothes and covering themselves with ashes. Ashes symbolized insignificance. Ashes are all that is left after the glory of fire.

The ashes we use tonight come from the palms we used last Palm Sunday—the day we wave branches in an almost defiant faith that welcomes Jesus into Jerusalem. Defiant, because we know Good Friday is coming, that Jesus will die; yet still we cheer his coming. What a paradox faith is! When we bury people, we commend their souls to God, acknowledging our mortality: "All of us go down to the dust; yet even at the grave we make our song: Alleluia, alleluia, alleluia." What a paradox faith is!

We are dust and to dust we shall return. This is, I think, what Joel and Jesus are after. All of our worship, all of our ritual comes down to this: In the end, none of it will save us. What will save us is our faith in God stored up in our hearts, not the material things that rust and turn to dust—just as we do. What a paradox faith is!

The Greek gods were said to envy our mortality, knowing that who could not *die* could not *love* with the same intensity, could not see the world charged with the same beauty as mortals do. Yet our God broke the bonds of immortality; came to live and die with us. What a paradox faith is!

Ours is a culture trying to pretend death does not happen, that if we could only find the right formula, we would live forever. And we are unprepared for death when it comes.

So, tonight, we will wear, above our eyes for all to see, over that place many traditions regard as the window of the soul, the most important public symbol of our faith: We are dust and yet, because of God, we live.

Mary Frances Schjonberg is Assistant Rector of Christ Church, Short Hills, New Jersey.

MAUNDY THURSDAY

Carter Brown's Gift

Exodus 12:1-14a; John 13:1-15
Mark Hollingsworth Jr.

PASSOVER AND MAUNDY THURSDAY. These two great observances of faith, celebrated around the world today, speak loudly of that for which we make space. They invite us to reflect on our availability to God, our openness to what God wants to bring us.

Through Moses and Aaron, God directed the children of Israel to make room in their lives for God to act, instructing them to gather as families, and to prepare a hasty meal of roasted lamb, unleavened bread, and bitter herbs; and to eat the meal hurriedly with loins girded, feet sandaled, staff in hand—packed and ready to go. Each family was instructed to mark the front door with the blood of the lamb, so that the spirit of God would pass over that house, sparing it from the plague intended for the Egyptians. This is a story about being available to God, making room for God to act; it is about readiness to receive grace, about responsiveness to the relentless generosity of God's love.

The story of Jesus' washing the disciples' feet on the night before he died addresses the same issue. So here, on Maundy Thursday, the one presiding at this service washes the feet of communicants, symbolically proclaiming the servanthood of God in Christ. It is a liturgical practice with which I have struggled. I first encountered it as a theological student, serving as a seminary intern in San Francisco. To a conservative son of New England it seemed contrived, this bathing of already well-scrubbed feet and drying them off with fluffy Cottonelle towels. It was particularly off-putting when the foot-washer brandished a pair of scissors to snip through the nylons worn by an ill-prepared foot-washee. It struck me as undignified—behavior inappropriate for church. It seemed particularly Californian.

Massey Shepherd, the great scholar and presbyter of the Church, a staid Southerner, allowed that he would consider washing on Maundy Thursday only the feet of any who had walked a considerable distance to church along dusty, dirt roads, barefoot.

I don't want someone washing my feet in church. It is too intimate, too personal. I am something of a prude. Thus I find great comfort in St. Peter's response to Jesus' invitation: *You will never wash my feet.* But very recently I have been helped to consider in a new light this thing that Jesus did and have been challenged to let it open me more fully to the intimacy God offers me in the process of my spiritual conversion. The help came from an extraordinary young friend.

When I met Carter Brown, he was a fifteen-year-old high school freshman fighting a particularly vicious form of cancer. The eldest of three boys, he was well over six feet tall, and loved all the things adolescent boys love—basketball, friends, music, boogie boarding. I met him shortly after his cancer had recurred and was attacking his bones. Over the course of our visits we talked for hours about the things in life that intrigued and delighted us. He asked me countless questions about myself—what foods, movies, and music I liked, what it was like being a priest, what it was like being an adoptive parent. It never felt like he was prying, rather that he was making a space for me in his life, and thereby a space for me in my own life, where I could just be who I am.

Carter was in and out of the hospital and the cancer clinic regularly because the disease in his bones was affecting his blood production and was extremely painful. But basically Carter was able to be at home, and during the day he lived on a couch in the living room, spending time with his family and friends. A couple of days before Carter died in early March, my six-year-old son and I were visiting with him. His parents and brothers were there. Friends came in and out. Carter was lying on the couch, under an old quilt. Though he was on considerable pain medication, the discomfort in his bones, especially his legs and his hips, made him move around a lot, as he tried in vain to get comfortable. All movement made the cuffs of his pajama pants ride up his long, thin legs, which made him more uncomfortable and a little chilly. So he asked me if I would help him. Lifting up the quilt, he asked me to pull the cuffs of his pajamas down so they would cover his aching legs. A simple request, but, making it, he made a place for me that defined our companionship as no words could. Allowing me to serve him in that seemingly insignificant way, he offered me a glimpse of the kind of intimacy God yearns to have with each of us.

On this Maundy Thursday, when I think of Jesus' hands gently washing the tired, sore feet of his disciples, I remember adjusting the legs of Carter Brown's pajamas, and drawing the soft, old quilt over his feet. And I wonder if I can make such a place for Jesus in my life. I wonder if I can let him get that close. I wonder if I can allow him to serve me. I wonder if I can be so available to God that I won't miss the precious, painful, glorious gifts God is ceaselessly trying to give me.

If I can't let Jesus wash my feet, how can I let him die for me?

Mark Hollingsworth Jr. is Archdeacon of the
Diocese of Massachusetts.

EASTER EVENING

Decorating the Easter Tree

Acts 5:29-33
Nancy Casey Fulton

THE LAST FEW YEARS I've noticed a proliferation of "Easter trees": living trees, their branches still bare, decorated with colorful eggs. Not too long ago, in a client's home, I saw a wooden Easter tree, beautifully decked out with tiny eggs, chickens, and rabbits in green, pink, and yellow. I have to admit, Easter trees don't capture my imagination the way Christmas trees do, so I've never had one. A few weeks ago, however, at a clergy conference, our presenter suggested that we don't know how to decorate the Easter tree. He showed us slides of his own family's Easter celebrations when he was a child. On one slide was an Easter tree standing bravely in the bare landscape of late winter. It took me a few minutes to realize that by "Easter tree," he meant the cross.

"We don't know how to decorate the cross": what an odd comment that seemed at the time. But I haven't been able to forget what he said, because I believe that his words strike at the heart of the problem Easter presents us. Compared to Easter, Christmas is a warm, fuzzy holy day— in spite of the baby Jesus being born to poor parents in a stable on a cold night, in spite of the threat to his infant life from Herod the King. Thanks to Luke, we have a sweet telling of the Holy Family, and at Christmas we gather with *our* families and deck out our houses with the warmth of greens, soft lights, and beautiful colors.

Easter isn't the same kind of holy day, coming as it does on the heels of Holy Week. The shadow of the cross is always at the corner of our vision. The wounds on Jesus' hands, feet, and side do not disappear with his Resurrection. We want to glory in the brilliant light surrounding the empty tomb, as well we should. The Resurrection should be a celebration.

But if we forget about the cross—the Easter tree—we are in danger of diminishing the triumph of Our Lord. And if we deck it out with nothing but the trappings of the secular world, we are in danger of forgetting what it means to be Christians. In our narthex we have placed the old cross that used to stand on top of this church. For Lent, we trimmed it simply with symbols of the Crucifixion: a crown of thorns, a whip, a purple chasuble draped to remind us of the cloak of Jesus. Last Sunday we added palms. And you might have noticed this morning that the Altar Guild has tucked some lily blossoms into the crown of thorns to remind us that Christ has risen. There is also a butterfly, placed there by the children at their Good Friday Stations of the Cross, to symbolize resurrection. Palms, crown of thorns, butterfly, and lilies tell us the story of Holy Week: the triumphant entry into Jerusalem, the terrible mockery and death, and the glorious victory over death. The hard reality of the cross stands in the midst of Easter joy, as it must.

You might also have noticed on the cross six purple squares of paper. The children who took part in the hands-on Stations of the Cross on Friday added their names, a reminder that they are part of Jesus' death and Resurrection, as are we all through our baptisms. Yes, we glory in the Resurrection, but that is only the beginning for us. Jesus reminded his followers that they must take up their crosses and follow him. We are given on this day the promise of eternal life, but also the burden of embracing the cross: we need to feel its weight, and feel its strength, for it empowers us to act in Jesus' name.

So how do we decorate the Easter tree? I've thought about that a lot this week as I've kept vigil with friends whose daughter was dying, and as I wrote a homily for her funeral yesterday. Do we hang her suffering and her parents' sorrow on the Easter tree? And the lost boys of the Sudan—many of them settling in Michigan—deprived of family and home through years of tribal warfare: do we hang their vulnerable bodies and souls on the Easter tree? And the young African-American man, shot dead when he ran from a police officer in Cincinnati not long ago: do we hang his senseless death, and his mother's grief, and his city's fear on the Easter tree? And Timothy McVeigh: do we hang his unrepentant spirit and the legal system's vengeance on the Easter tree?

If we truly decorate the Easter tree, it will display all the pain of the world, as well as all the joy. It will display the crown of thorns as well as the lily blossoms. And it will display each of us, for we are inheritors of both the suffering and the joy. Last evening at the Vigil service we read a children's version of the creation story concluding with this sentence: "Then the angels asked God, 'Is the world finished yet?' and God answered, 'I don't know. Go ask my partners.'" The work of creation, the work of redemption, the work of fulfilling the promise of the Resurrection goes on through us. That is the beauty of the Easter tree. May the cross of Jesus strengthen us and open our hearts, and may the radiance of the Resurrection shine without end in our lives and in our world.

Nancy Casey Fulton is Rector of St. John's Church,
Mount Pleasant, Michigan.

DAY OF PENTECOST

Hurricane Season

Acts 2:1-11; John 20:19-31
Margaret S. Austin

TWO NEW SEASONS begin this weekend: hurricane season, which runs through the end of November, and the season of Pentecost, which this year coincides with hurricane season. As people who value coastal life, we know too well what happens when a hurricane blasts into our lives. Survival mode takes over. We gather everyone and everything we need to keep us alive and safe. We hunker down, anchor ourselves against the threatening forces. Whatever our safe places, we feel trapped—afraid to leave, afraid to stay. We board ourselves in with plywood and tape, surround ourselves with sandbags, and sit in the middle of the house. Even then we know we are relatively helpless against the winds that pitch and boil, the ocean's waters that damage or demolish our most substantial human constructions.

It was August. I was focused on launching my sophomore year of college. Freshman year had been awesome. For the first time in twelve years I had cast off the navy skirt, white blouse, and black-and-white saddle oxfords of Catholic school, and taken on short skirts, red sweaters, and Bass Weejuns. Boys and girls, previously contained in separate schoolrooms, were young men and women sharing cafeteria tables and classrooms. We were old enough to vote, drink, and make decisions about what we did, where we went, and with whom. Intoxicating stuff–this threshold of freedom!

New relationships were risked that first year, especially among roommates. Some four-girl suites had exploded before the first term papers were handed in; others had shaken successfully through the sifter of disparateness. Our quartet hung in between. The "hitch in our git along" was Linda. Brilliant, diligent, microbiology major Linda. Strangely clothed, overweight, always dateless Linda.

The first day of freshman year she arrived in a cab after the long flight from a part of the country none of us had even thought about. When the rest of us headed home for turkey, dressing, and cranberry sauce, Linda "decided" to stay on campus to do some lab work or something. Although she announced plans to stick around and clean up some term papers over the Christmas holiday, at the eleventh hour, Jane, trying to be nice but hoping for a turn-down, invited Linda to spend Christmas at her house. When they returned, Jane declared that Christmas break had been a disaster.

In the Deep South of the early '60s, we were not considerate of one another's uniqueness. More than a few times Linda heard our catty whispering, caught our eyes rolling as she plopped on the floor and strummed out Peter, Paul, and Mary tunes, while the rest of us flitted around, shrieking about football games, parties, boyfriends, and summer plans. Sometimes not so secretly, we hoped Linda would not return after the summer break. We wanted her to find another suite, at least, leaving space in ours for somebody really cool, more like us.

In August, as my dad and I were sitting in the kitchen fine-tuning the trek to return me to co-ed splendor, he grabbed the telephone before it finished one ring. It was Linda's mom. Concerned about how the gathering strength and rapid movement of Hurricane Betsy might affect Linda's return to school for registration, she wanted a first-hand update on the approaching storm. Daddy filled her in, and, before I could stop him, he insisted that Linda come on the next flight, whereupon we *(we?!)* would meet her at the airport and take her to our house where "she and Margaret can spend the week talking roommate talk and getting ready to go back to school." No matter that I was mouthing a silent scream: "DADDY! NOOO!" My fate was sealed. Linda and Hurricane Betsy were on the way.

At first, Linda and I sat on the front porch or walked around the neighborhood, the wind hardly disturbing our straight blonde hair. We talked about storms, college courses, music, TV shows. Safe impersonal stuff. But the dark and dangerous eye of the storm was focused right on New Orleans. By the time Betsy began to show what she was made of, Linda and I had run out of conversation. It was just as well; my entire household had kicked into survivor mode—filling water containers, stocking canned foods, lining up candles and batteries, boarding windows. The forceful winds and relentless rain slammed against our house for hours as we hunkered down in various close spaces.

In the dark and frightful confines of my room, Linda began to cry. Her tears were born not of the storm outside, but of the storm of her life, which she unpacked in painful detail through the black and noisy night of Hurricane Betsy. The rain-swollen bayous emptied into the streets, and the water outside our house reached perilous levels while Linda described life with not one but two parents awash in alcohol. Huge tree branches crashed against the roof as Linda lined up the broken sticks of her life, cracked and snapped in the screaming slugfests that were routine in her existence. The howling wind pummeled my house, threatening to blow the windows and doors in, while the blast of misery from Linda's life blew through my head and my heart with equal force. I wanted it all to stop. I wanted to stay in the relative safety of my dark but familiar room, and I wanted to run as far as I could from what was happening within it. I wanted to run from the intensity of storms I had not come close to imagining.

By late morning, Betsy allowed us to view our surroundings as she had so savagely rearranged them. It was clear from first glance that the neat and familiar landscape of my neighborhood would never be the same, that it would take a lifetime of hard work and cooperation between neighbors and nature for life to be viable again.

I believe this is what Pentecost was like for the apostles, and is for us. We are often trapped in life, by too many good things or too many bad things. Afraid to leave and afraid to stay, we are helpless, and we move into survival mode. Pentecost marks the descent of the Holy Spirit of God—a spirit different from our own (that's what *holy* means—different). Different from human nature, which is wont to create comfortable, exclusive, internal universes.

The Holy Spirit of God is not some spooky religious foolishness, not a spiritual crutch. It is the profound but simple gift of God's power to understand each other, to accept each other, to forgive each other. It is the hurricane-like wind that, if we have the courage to conspire with it, will rearrange us into people who can be more than we are, and do more than we do—not just for ourselves, but for others. It is the earth-shaking blast that affords us power to choose love instead of hate, acceptance over judgment.

By our senior year, Linda had met and married a great guy. My mom made her wedding dress. I was her maid of honor; later, she was mine. All because of the pushiness of the wind. God, you see, breathes life into you and me through a mighty rush of wind, because nothing less will get the job done. The surge of spirit wind scares the hell out of us and propels us out of the upper room and into the dormitory room, the classroom, the boardroom, the courtroom, the hospital waiting room. The uninvited, undeserved, unexpected storm of God's loving breath: it is our life's work to inhale it, so that we might exhale and give new life to others. It is our life's work to enable the fierce, frightening, freeing breath of God to empower us to think what God thinks, to feel what God feels, to want what God wants, and to do what God does.

"When it was evening on that day . . . and the doors of the house where the disciples had met were locked for fear . . . Jesus came and stood among them and said, 'Peace be with you . . . As the Father has sent me, so I send you . . .' When he had said this, he breathed on them and said to them, "Receive the Holy Spirit."

Margaret S. Austin is Associate Rector of St. Stephen's Church, Richmond, Virginia.

TRINITY SUNDAY

Experiencing the Trinity

John 3:1-16
Alicia Schuster-Weltner

SHAMROCKS. Fleur-de-lis. Fish swimming in an endless circle. A triangle inside a circle. All symbols for the Trinity, because words are never enough. Pictures that try to show what cannot be told. All our words over the centuries have only touched the edges of this foundation of our faith. Father, Son, and Holy Spirit—words that are more than words can explain, more than minds can fathom. The Trinity is inexplicable, finally, just as the person we love most is inexplicable. But that has never stopped us from trying to explore and experience the loving relationship that is God. The Trinity enters our lives like chords of music, each a separate note, but in need of the others.

Fourteenth-century mystic Julian of Norwich said of the Trinity, "God showed me something small, no bigger than a hazelnut, lying in the palm of my hand . . . In this little thing I saw three properties. The first is that God made it, the second is that God loves it, and the third is that God preserves it . . . God is the Creator and the protector and the lover. . . . Just as the blessed Trinity made all things out of nothing, so the same blessed Trinity shall make good all that is not well."[1]

---

1. Julian of Norwich, *Showings*, trans. Edmund Colledge, O.S.A., and James Walsh, S.J. (New York: Paulist Press, 1978), 183, 232-33.

In 1906, weeks before her death at twenty-six, Elizabeth of the Trinity, a French Carmelite nun, wrote of the "merciful Trinity": "the place where the Son of God is hidden is in the bosom of the Father . . . invisible to every mortal eye, unattainable by every human intellect. . . . And yet his will is that we should be established in him, that we should live where he lives, in the unity of love. . . . The Trinity. That is our dwelling, our home, the Father's house that we must never leave."[2]

And Kathleen Norris, in her poem "Kitchen Trinity," says: "Three women at a table hold the world. One gets up to stir the stars, one makes the fire, another blows on it to keep it going."[3] Particle physics revolutionized the scientific world when it was discovered that atoms, microscopically small as they are, contain not just ever smaller particles, but also vast amounts of empty space. Matter is not solid, but open. I wonder if the Trinity does not contain empty space, too, space between Father, Son, and Holy Spirit—there for us to dwell in, to love, work, and fail in, there for us to wander and wail in, never, ultimately, lost. There is space in the love of God, in the Trinity, for us to dwell in, space enclosing us, in ways true and touchable.

I am most clear about the Trinity when I look at my sleeping daughter, who will soon be one year old. Reflected in her face I see a peace I can only begin to understand but which I recognize as the miracle of creation. When I listen to her quiet breathing, I feel the Spirit not just as a wind, even a holy one, but as the life-giving and healing breath.

When Sally was nine days old, she was hospitalized with a mysterious fever. The doctors didn't know the origin, and because the possible causes of fever at that age are life threatening, we spent the next five days in a blur of tests, IVs, antibiotics, and feeding tubes. Finally, the fever left, the worst causes were ruled out, and we went home bewildered, exhausted, more than a little fearful of the future.

I remember holding tiny baby Sally and praying every prayer I could remember. One came from somewhere in the depths of my mind, a version of the hymn, "St. Patrick's Breastplate." After all my study

---

2. Elizabeth of the Trinity, *The Complete Works*, vol. 1., *Major Spiritual Writings*, trans. Aletheia Kane, O.C.D. (Washington: ICS Publications, 1984), 94.

3. In Kathleen Norris, *Little Girls in Church* (Pittsburgh: University of Pittsburgh Press, 1955), 14.

and thinking, all my wanderings of heart and mind around the Trinity, sitting in that glider by the window, rocking, I knew why it mattered. The Trinity became for me more than a word or a symbol.

"I bind unto myself today the strong name of the Trinity," I prayed. I knew that I was praying to a Father who knew the pain I was enduring as a mother. Praying to a Son whose pain and suffering hallowed all the pain my daughter endured, all my worries and my breaking heart. Praying to a Spirit who gave me strength to go on. I knew that I was wonderfully trapped by God, enclosed, loved by the Trinity. I knew I had nothing to fear, that all would somehow be well, that I was being held by God as closely as I held my baby daughter.

I know you have experienced this too. The Trinity has loved you here, where we enter each Sunday under an icon to the same. The Trinity loves you in this place that fire almost destroyed and yet made fully new again—a place that since 1892 has witnessed to the power of God to shape and transform hearts, a power even now waiting to begin its newest chapter.

And the Trinity has loved you in places in your own hearts where God most closely dwells, loved you when you were too lost and defeated to go on. The Father has mothered you and rocked you close, when you were too tired to walk toward tomorrow. The Son has taken your arm and held you up. When you were too frightened to hope, the Spirit has consoled you and strengthened you, giving you breath you didn't know you had. In all these times the Trinity has loved you.

I thank God for all of you, because you have helped me to know the love of the Trinity along with you. I know now in a way I never did before that I am surrounded by the love of God because of the way you have loved my family and me, the way you love and care for one another, the way you reach out to the hurt, hungry, and helpless. Because the Trinity has loved us, we are still here as a church and as a people. We have survived when we might have perished and loved when we might have hated. We have stayed when we might have left. We have persevered when we might have given up.

What a thought; to know that the Trinity, as much a mystery as it will always remain to us, is not a problem but a place in which we already dwell, and a God big enough to embrace all our endings and beginnings. The Trinity has loved us and taught us to love. And so we love on, knowing in whose space we dwell, and that indeed, all shall be well.

Alicia Schuster-Weltner is Assistant Rector of St. Martin-in-the-Fields Church, Atlanta, Georgia.

THE PRESENTATION OF OUR LORD

Anna's Wisdom

Luke 2:22-40
Richard L. Ullman

THE FEAST OF the Presentation is a lovely grace note in the Church's calendar. It marks the poignant day when Mary presented herself to the priests in the Temple in Jerusalem for purification forty days after childbirth. When she presented herself, she presented her baby also, obedient to the Lord's command in that every firstborn son should be dedicated to God in memory of Israel's deliverance from slavery in Egypt.

St. Luke tells us two devout elderly people were in the Temple to witness the Presentation: Anna, whom Luke calls a prophetess, and pious old Simeon, whose poetic words have been sung for ages ever since: "Lord, you now have set your servant free to go in peace as you have promised." Because of this beautiful song, Simeon is the more famous of the witnesses. But Anna has a special place in my heart because of another Anna, a member of the parish I served during the 1970s. There is someone like her in almost every congregation: always present, but on the fringes, and just a little, shall we say, "off key."

I was heading back to the rectory after Good Friday services. As I passed by the main entrance of the church, there was Anna. She and her daughter were poking about in the garden nestled in the corner where the entranceway joins the main wall of the building.

"Hello, Anna," I said.

"Hello, Rector. We came too late for the Good Friday service. But this is even better. See these stones we've found here by the church wall? They come from the Holy Land. These are stones that Jesus sent. We're going to take them home, and be with Jesus for Good Friday."

Anna stopped talking. She looked me straight in the eye. Clearly it was my turn to say something, but my brain just whirred and whirred, with no result. "That's nice," was all my tongue could find to say.

"You don't mind if we take the stones, do you, Rector? That's even better than going to the Good Friday service, don't you think?"

"Oh, fine, Anna," said I. "Take all the stones you want." And I walked, wondering, on home.

My next major encounter with Anna was a couple of years later, when her husband called me one cold fall night. Anna was wandering the streets of her neighborhood in nothing but her nightgown. Their son had persuaded her to sit down in the breezeway. Would I come and try to help? I did, and Anna agreed to let me take her to the mental health clinic. Over the next several weeks she began to feel much better, but she never again found holy stones in the church garden.

I believe the prophetess Anna of today's Gospel may have been very much like my Anna of the Good Friday Jesus stones. Anna of the Feast of the Presentation was married in her teens and became a childless widow in her early twenties. For six long decades she bore God only knows what burdens of loneliness and pain. She came to the Temple every day: always there, ever on the fringes, undoubtedly often out of phase with whatever festival or fast was being observed.

She began her widow's watch about the time that Pompey defeated the last of the heirs of Alexander the Great. The great general made Syria, then Galilee and Judah, part of the Roman Empire, marching with his army into Jerusalem; Anna was there. Her watch continued as Julius Caesar rose to power. The first Caesar established the first of the Herods as puppets of Rome; Anna was there. Night and day she prayed and fasted at the Temple. Herod the Great captured Jerusalem, became king, and rebuilt the city, including the Temple and its precincts, meanwhile committing all manner of tyrannical atrocities; Anna was there.

In season and out, the widow kept her watch. When, one day, she saw a couple approaching with their infant, who can tell exactly what went on within her heart? There was the woman, barely past girlhood, accompanied by her clearly older husband. Did Anna's mind flash back sixty years to her younger self, the husband of her too-brief marriage, and the baby she longed for but never had? And what did she think of the baby now before her, warmly held hope, future in flesh?

Tradition does not preserve her words, only that she responded. All Luke says is, "At that moment she came, and began to praise God and to speak about the child to all who were looking for the redemption of Jerusalem." Perhaps her words were incoherent. But surely you and I know her meaning:

"O, praise God! Look at that!
A mother and father and child! A holy family!

Blessed hope, now in flesh appearing.
After all the seasons of pain I have seen, I do now know that God will
    yet bring redemption to his suffering people.
God love that baby! God love poor, old Anna.
God love Israel."

No matter what Anna said—and there is no doubt that her words
lacked the polish and poetry of venerable Simeon's Song—no matter what
Anna said, that's what she meant. That was the sweet fruit of her long
and weary widow's watch. And for that beautiful, nurturing fruit, Luke
records her name and we remember Anna today.

Over and over I am struck how God uses the marginal, the weak, the
fragile to speak wisdom and truth. Anna of the Feast of the Presentation
is the saint for all who are marginal, or weak, or fragile. Indeed, she is
the saint for all that is marginal and weak and fragile within the heart
and soul and mind of each of us! Thank God for Anna and her margin-
alized, weak, and fragile sisters and brothers. Thank God for all the
Annas who bear messages of God's love and strengthening presence,
whether in the pebbles of a church garden or in the flesh of an infant
longed for but never seen, save in another mother's arms.

O, praise God!
Look at that! Stones from the Holy Land, sent by Jesus! A holy family!
Blessed hope! After all the seasons of pain I have seen, I do now know
    that God will yet bring redemption to his suffering people.
Treasure those stones; love that baby!
God love poor, old Anna.
God love Israel.

And God love both you and me, gracing us with ears to hear and hearts
to listen to every Anna's wisdom.

*Richard L. Ullman, now retired, was Rector of Trinity Church,
Toledo, Ohio, and Archdeacon of the Diocese of Southern Ohio.*

ASCENSION DAY

Understanding Is the Booby Prize

Ezekiel 1:3-5a, 15-22, 26-28; Luke 24:49-53
James Bradley

THE ASCENSION is a difficult concept for twenty-first-century folks. We are challenged by the "spatiality" of the Ascension. We do not live in the three-layered, pre-Copernican universe. What is *up there* isn't a heaven surrounding the earth like a canopy. We all know that what's up there is "the vast expanse of interstellar space" of "galaxies, suns, and planets in their courses."

For most of us, God's Eternal Kingdom isn't a physical *place*. I suspect our understanding of "heaven" is fuzzy and undefined at best. So the image of Jesus beginning to levitate upwards toward the sky to join the God he called Father defies not only the law of gravity, but human reason as well. Yet we must deal with the Ascension story—"embrace" the Ascended Christ even if we don't "understand" it.

A friend of mine often says, "Understanding is the booby prize." Understanding is so much a part of our lives that we will often sacrifice truth for mere comprehension. Truth is not a faculty of the intellect— truth belongs to the heart. If we are to embrace the Ascension story we must do so with our hearts.

But before we tackle the Ascension, let's look at the lesson from Ezekiel. Ezekiel's vision was a theophany, a peek through the veil, a look behind the curtain, a vision of God—a vision of wheels within wheels. It sounds like a psychotic event, or something out of science fiction. Whatever it was, it would challenge the special effects of Steven Spielberg and George Lucas to make it visual for us. Whatever it was, it would have been beyond our comprehension, beyond the limits of our understanding. Whatever it was, it was not of this world. Ezekiel's reaction was to "fall on his face."

When I was a little boy in Sunday school in the Methodist Church in West Virginia, I was always impressed by how people in the Bible would fall on their faces. It happened a lot. What I thought back then was that the people were kneeling down to worship, not like us Episcopalians, but like Muslims—all the way down on the ground, their faces in their prayer rugs.

It was years before I realized that they weren't choosing to kneel down at all. When people come face to face with the Holy—what Rudolph Otto calls "the *mysterium tremendum*"—when people came face to face with God, they are literally "knocked off their feet."

The Holy does that to you. One minute you're standing up, trying to understand, and the next minute you're prone on the ground—flat on your face, knocked out by God.

In Sunday school I learned a song about Ezekiel and his vision: *Ezekiel saw a wheel, way up in the middle of the air./A wheel within a wheel, way up in the middle of the air./The big wheel runs on faith and the little wheel runs on the grace of God./A wheel within a wheel, way up in the middle of the air.* That isn't a song about understanding. It's a song about embracing. That's what we need to do to on the Feast of the Ascension.

The English word *ascend* has a fascinating derivation. It comes from the Latin *ad scandere*, literally, "to climb up." But the Latin verb *scandere* is also the root word of the English word *scan*. We all know what it means to "scan" something when we're reading. We don't read every word, but skip and jump from word to word, trying to get the gist of the meaning. The Latin root of *scandere* can be traced all the way back to Sanskrit—the mother language of all Indo-European tongues. The Sanskrit verb is *skan-da-ti*, literally, "he leaps."

In Luke's Gospel, Jesus leaps out of this world into the Kingdom, out of this reality into another reality. Jesus leaps to his Father; he leaps to his God and our God. It is a leap of the heart far beyond our understanding.

But for me, the really interesting thing is how Jesus got to the "jumping-off place" in Bethany. Listen: "Jesus said to his disciples, 'And see, I am sending upon you what my Father promised; so stay here in the city until you have been clothed with power from on high.' Then he led them out as far as Bethany. . . ."

From the Gospel account, we know this: after the Crucifixion, the disciples returned to the place where they had been with Jesus on Maundy Thursday. They returned to that upper room and locked the doors in fear. The room where they had celebrated the Last Supper with Jesus became their "safe house" after he was killed. It is to the same room that he came to his friends and followers after his Resurrection. So when Luke tells us "he led them out as far as Bethany," we can imagine that they began from that place—where they had been for their final earthly meal with Jesus. In fact, just a few verses before today's Gospel lesson, Jesus eats with them again. He asks them if they have anything to eat, and they give him a piece of fish.

Remember what happened after the Last Supper? Jesus led the disciples out from the house where they shared the meal, down through the Kidron Valley, and up the hill to the Garden of Gethsemane where he prayed and was arrested. Bethany is on the other side of the hill from Gethsemane. So the journey he led them on before his ascension was the very journey they had made with him before. It was a case of *déjà vu* for the disciples. They had all been here before.

So the journey to the cross and the journey to ascension were the same journey. Jesus' followers walked familiar ground. They knew the way "by heart." The first trip saw Jesus leap onto the cross. The second trip saw him leap out of this world back to God. It was nearly the same jumping-off place. Astounding!

And here is what I think is true—you and I must take a leap of faith this night. It's not an easy thing for twenty-first-century rationalists like you and me. We are more likely to avoid the high places altogether rather than leaping off. Yet that is what the Feast of the Ascension asks of us. To leap, to let go, to fall free into the heart of God.

There was a man who climbed a high mountain he never dreamed he could climb. At the summit, he looked around—transfixed by the beauty of the view from so high a place. In his excitement and wonder, he ventured too near the edge of the pinnacle and slipped off. Miraculously, he grabbed hold of a branch growing inexplicably out of the side of the sheer mountain wall. So he hung suspended, hundreds of feet above a jumble of rocks, with no way to save himself. Though he knew no one else was on the mountaintop, he called out for a long time for help. When that hope was exhausted, he looked up to the heavens and cried, "Can anyone up there save me?"

Much to his surprise, a voice answered, "Yes, I can save you." The man's heart filled with hope. "Tell me what to do," he cried out to the sky. "I'll give all I have to the poor. I'll become a missionary and go to unknown lands. I'll do anything you ask if you will just save me." The voice replied, "Well, all you have to do is let go of that branch." There was a long, pregnant silence. The man tightened his grip on the branch and called out, "Is there anyone *else* up there who can save me?"

Jesus leaped onto the cross and then leaped out of the tomb and then leaped back to the Father. And this night of the celebration of Christ's ascension, we are asked to leap as well. We are called to make a leap of faith—to forgo understanding and embrace the ascending Christ in our hearts. We are called to let go of whatever branch keeps us stuck and trust in the power of God to save us. *The big wheel runs on faith and the little wheel runs on the grace of God.*

It's that kind of night—a night of wonder, astonishment, and hope. We need to "let go" and embrace God with our hearts. We need to fall on our faces in the presence of the Holy. We need to take the leap, trusting we will fall into the very heart of God. Understanding, on this night, is the "booby prize." Trust your heart. Trust God. Jump.

James Bradley is Rector of St. John on the Green, Waterbury, Connecticut.

THE TRANSFIGURATION OF OUR LORD

Seeing Things as They Really Are

Luke 9:28-36
Ralph Carskadden

THE BRILLIANT LIGHT was seen high in the morning sky. At first there was silence. Then a tremendous sound. Then a searing heat, vaporizing wood and flesh. The garments of those at a distance from the epicenter were burned off the bodies of the wearers, the patterns of cloth appearing like cosmic tattoos on the flesh underneath. The earth itself was sterilized with heat and radiation. In little home gardens on the perimeter of the blast site, the potatoes in the ground were roasted. Seventy thousand people, mostly civilians—older adults and young children—died instantly or within hours. Thousands more died slow, painful deaths over the following days, weeks, and years.

The bomb was the product of the so-called "Trinity Project." The atom bomb was exploded over a civilian target on The Feast of the Transfiguration, fifty years ago.

The moral debate over the use of the atomic and hydrogen bombs continues to this day. Most suggest that since the evil enemies of democracy had committed atrocities, we were justified in taking such means to stop them. Precedent had been set when the Allies firebombed Dresden and Berlin. After that, it seemed logical to undertake wholesale destruction of civilian targets on other cities such as Hiroshima and Nagasaki.

The brilliant unearthly light in the sky, the awesome roar from the heavens, the consuming fire, and the invisible but lethal radiation that destroyed and disfigured humans, animals, and earth itself—these are memories of humankind's power unleashed against itself and against creation.

But August sixth has other memories, memories dating back not just fifty years, but twenty centuries: memories of radiant light, heavenly voice, and transfigured human. Tradition calls the place of Transfiguration Mount Tabor. Jesus had taken his closest friends, Peter, James, and John to an isolated place for prayer. He was on his way to Jerusalem where he would run head-on into the religious and political powers—a run-in that would lead to his death. He had gone to the mountain for perspective, for silence. As often occurred on such occasions, he entered into deep prayer, and his friends fell asleep.

When they awoke, they saw him standing, talking with Moses, the liberator and lawgiver of God's people, and with Elijah, the greatest of the prophets, who had been taken into the heavens in a chariot of fire and was expected to return someday, to herald the coming of the Messiah and the beginning of God's reign of justice. As he spoke with Moses and Elijah about his own approaching exodus, Jesus was enveloped with brilliant light. His face shone, his garments glowed.

And that light was reflected in everything; that brilliance, that transfiguring radiance spilled over into the faces and garments of the disciples. It spilled over onto the ground itself, the rocks, the plants, the trees, and flowers. The entire creation was seen to be alive. It was not a light that blinded; it illumined everything. In that light everyone and everything could be seen in its true essence. Its true beauty, its purpose, place, and relationship with everything and everyone else was somehow for a moment seen, really seen. And then a cloud passed over, hiding the brilliance for a moment, a cloud covering the presence of the Living God, who spoke: "This is my Son, my Chosen. Listen to him!" And when the cloud had passed, Jesus was alone.

What happened on the mountain that day? Did Jesus really change? Or were Jesus and creation always that way, and only on that occasion did the disciples have the eyes of faith to see?

Today the anniversary of Hiroshima invites us to see ourselves, members of the human race, as we are, as we really are: capable of using power to destroy, to control, to subjugate, to terrorize, to keep in place those who are thought to be less. Capable in our blindness of using other creatures and creation itself as things, endless resources to waste without consequence.

But today the Feast of the Transfiguration invites us to see ourselves also as we are, really are, and to see each other and creation with the eyes of the disciples, who for a moment glimpsed the divine presence within each other and the whole creation. Today in the presence of Moses, Elijah, and Jesus, we see how power can be used to serve, liberate, forgive, to bring out and up those who have been put down.

And today at her baptism into Christ we are invited to see Emily as she really is, created in the image and likeness of God. Today we have come to a mountain ridge to join her in prayer. Today we hear the divine voice calling her by name. Today the Spirit will illumine and enlighten her. Today before our eyes we will see her buried and raised in Christ.

Marcel Proust wrote: "The real voyage of discovery consists not in seeking new lands, but in seeing with new eyes." If we see the events of this morning with new eyes, we will see that into the water of baptism Emily will carry humankind's memories of Cain and Abel, of Battan and the stalags, of Auschwitz and Nanking, of Pearl Harbor and Okinawa, of Hiroshima and Nagasaki, of Cape Town and Ngara, of Shebernitza and Port au Prince. With new eyes we will also see that in the waters of baptism Emily will discover herself on holy ground. She will be washed in the primal water of creation and restored as God made her and intended her; she will pass through the waters of the Red Sea into the new life of freedom with Moses and the children of Israel; in the water of baptism she will cross over the Jordan and enter the promised life in God's kingdom of peace, justice, and righteousness.

This is the reality we are invited to behold on this day!

Ralph Carskadden is Rector of St. Clement's Church,
Seattle, Washington.

ALL SAINTS' DAY

Companions

Ecclesiasticus 44:1-10, 13-14; Revelation 7:2-4, 9-17
Carol Westpfahl

IT WAS BOXING DAY, December twenty-sixth. My friend had flown into London on the twenty-fourth, to celebrate my first Christmas in England. Most of England was still at home, polishing off leftover plum pudding and Christmas cake. But with the excitement and energy of twenty-five-year-olds on adventure, we'd gotten up early and driven to Durham. My friend had gone to shop. I went to Durham Cathedral, which has some of the oldest construction in Britain. It is immense, all in stone, with thick walls and massive pillars. The floor is wavy, worn by a thousand years of feet walking across its stones.

Although it was mid-afternoon, it was dusky twilight—typical of the far north in December. The cathedral is too old for Gothic arches or big windows. The only light was the glow from the lights strung on a Christmas tree, placed near the grave of St. Cuthbert behind the altar. I tucked myself in a corner, under an arch near the monks' meeting room, and closed my eyes. The stone felt smooth and solid against my back. The air smelled like old wax and rain. I just rested. Eventually I began to catch snatches of song—Gregorian chant it seemed—floating out of the corridor behind me. I started to picture the passages, wondering where the music might be coming from. As I visualized different parts of the cathedral, I began to see people in them—dressed in the old clothes we'd seen earlier in some historical exhibits. There were monks, peasants, and clergy, all busy about various tasks.

The pictures broadened. I saw more people. Some were handing things to others. Eventually I realized there was a progression going on. I was watching generations of monks, townspeople, and clergy work, pray, and study in the cathedral. Each had their time, then handed the work on to the next group. I started to realize that a long line of connections allowed me to sit in the church that day. From its inception, people of each generation had worked to be faithful in whatever challenges they faced. When their time was finished, they were able to pass the fruit of their labors to the next generation. Because all had done their part, the church still stood, after a thousand years. The people of my day could enter and worship the God who'd been glorified there for centuries, because of the faithfulness of people who had come before. I felt grateful to all those people for what their hard work had given me. I felt united to them, linked through all those generations.

When my friend came and found me, she asked why I was smiling. At the time, I'd never even heard the phrase. Later, I realized that this was my first experience of the communion of saints.

Today we celebrate All Saints' Day. Through it we remind ourselves of several things about saints, and about ways in which we are connected to one another and God. Our commemoration began with readings that offer us two visions, each with a different vantage point about holiness, faithfulness, and the ways of God.

Ben Sira, scribe and the writer of Ecclesiasticus, shouts his summons across the centuries, "Let us now sing the praises of famous men . . ." and goes on to commend kings, scholars, prophets, and artists. But just as we are settling down to hear a rousing tale of noble deeds and outstanding accomplishments, Ben throws us a curve. There are others too, he tells us. They also did great things, and we don't remember them, but their names persist. They and their children have perished, but their offspring live on.

This raises questions: If you admit you don't remember someone, how can their name persist? If a person's children have perished, how can their offspring live on? The scribe helps us sort it out. "These also were godly men, whose righteous deeds have not been forgotten." Aah—these people do live on, but not through their human children. Their offspring are the works they did as followers of God.

We've just started to chew on that when John shows up. He wants to tell us about the visions he's having. He has seen the servants of God. First he tries to describe 144,000 people, an astounding number in his time. Then even that is not enough—the followers of the Lamb are a great multitude, he says, more than anyone can count, from every tribe, people, language, and nation. Again, we have a question: Why does the number matter?

Like Ben Sira, John helps us sort it out. The multitude is uncountable, because it is *everybody*.

In John's revelation, we are all members of that crowd. Not only does it hold the peoples from all languages, and all nations, but also from all of history. We are all the saints of God.

And so there are two dynamics to our feast today. Every person has his or her own role to play in the reign of God, work to fulfill and hand on to the generations that follow. All Saints' celebrates the grace in each life that pours forth that person's unique witness to God. Then there is also the community—all of us, linked together throughout time and beyond. This great web of connection to others, past, present, and future, helps us to offer our faithful service. We are encouraged, supported, and sustained to do the work we were created to do. We are each called to the Christian life in a unique way, yet we are not alone. We live out our own version within a community, a web of connection that we call the communion of saints.

Shortly we will approach this table to fulfill Jesus' command to "do this in remembrance of me." As we do that, we come to our ultimate celebration of All Saints' Day, "remembering his death and resurrection." To re-member is to become a member again, to reconnect. With these words, the lid is blown off time. The past is brought into the present, the eternal now. We are tied to all who have ever offered this prayer before us, bound together with all throughout history who have shared the cup. We are united through the future to the heavenly banquet, when the feasting will never end. In the midst of that celebrating, while moving beyond time, we are joined by the communion of saints.

We may not be able to see them, but they are here—people from throughout the ages who have followed God. A huge crowd, as large as John described. Some we know about—Francis, and King Edmund, and Martin Luther King. Others have stories we've never heard. There are almond-eyed Ethiopians, pale Norwegians, and those who spent their lives on the slopes of the Andes. Some are recent arrivals. We will read their names today and celebrate their lives among us. Those among the communion of saints are our companions in the fullest sense of the word. They are those with whom we have shared bread—*com pan*—the bread on this altar which sustains us for the work we've been made to do. Let us join the banquet.

Carol Westpfahl is a priest in the Diocese of Olympia.

3

THE CONFESSION OF SAINT PETER

The Biography of Confession

Matthew 16:13-19
Nora Gallagher

PETER HAS ALWAYS been one of my favorite disciples because he is so human—forever getting it wrong. He walks on water for a few minutes, looks down at that deep lake and those terrifying waves, loses all confidence, and nearly drowns. At the Transfiguration, he announces he will build three shelters so they can all stay on that high hill forever. And it's Peter who, at the last hour, betrays his love for Jesus by denying that he knows him.

I can see myself in Peter. I have faith for a few minutes, and then allow fear and defensive reactions to overwhelm me. When I experience God's glory, I just want to stay there. Hang out. I don't want to go down into the streets and risk muddying it up with human affairs. And I am sure that I would do exactly as Peter did in Jerusalem. I am a coward, too.

But there is also the wonderful Peter, the man who abandons his fishing boat to follow this teacher. He's willing to act on a hunch. He is often the one who asks Jesus to explain or clarify what he is saying. And he is the one bold enough to say to Jesus, "You are the Messiah, the Son of the Living God." How does Peter come to know this is the Messiah? How do we come to know who is the Christ in our lives?

When we read the story about Jesus walking on the water, we must remember what precedes it. Jesus has just fed five thousand people on a few loaves and two fish. Peter has witnessed this event. Those of us who have worked in a soup kitchen, when we managed to stretch a crate of rotting vegetables and make a delicious soup, have felt that sudden realization of God's abundance. How wonderful to know there is always enough, if we just manage to share! Our souls slip forth in those moments, as Mary Oliver says, "like a tremor of pure sunlight."[1] Peter

---

1. Mary Oliver, *New and Selected Poems* (Boston: Beacon Press, 1992), 97-98; reprinted by permission.

must have felt something like that, a sense of how the world could be different, more abundant, more lovely than he had ever imagined.

The next thing he knows, he's out in a boat on a lake at night. The disciples, battling a head wind and a rough sea, are miserable, sleepy, and exhausted. In those hours of the night between three and six when, if we wake, we are at our lowest, our most anxious, Jesus walks toward them on the water. Peter, in terror, no doubt, asks him to prove himself. If it's you, he says, tell me to come to you. And, bad news for Peter, that's exactly what Jesus does. When has this happened to us? When have we said to Jesus, if it's you, call out to me? And when have we been astonished and terrified by the answer? Jesus says to Peter, "Come," a tender, demanding word. It is that answer that makes us afraid, not our question. It is Jesus' tenderness that is, as Oliver says, "a thousand times more frightening/ than the killer sea."

What is our water? When the women of the base community at Mission Dolores in Los Angeles read this gospel, they decided their water was the night around the projects, and the gangs that took over the night streets. They decided to "walk on water" by going out into the night together in groups and "taking it back." They reclaimed the streets. Certainly our water must be those things we are most sure we cannot do. And somehow, the doing of them breaks us into a new life, brings us closer to knowing who we are. Often, I think it is those moments when we "come out of the closet." It is about admitting to others, maybe even to ourselves, something we have known for years, and been afraid to say. I remember when I began to tell my friends, "Yes, I do go to church. Yes, I am trying to believe in God."

Then of course, Peter slips. He feels the strength of the wind. He cries out. Surely, so have we—sensed God's strength, God's ability to hold us up even on water. We have experienced, like those women at Mission Dolores, just how far we can go. We have seen possibility. And then our defenses return. Barriers go up. Old habits die hard. We sink into the waves. This is the rhythm, the torturous rhythm of life. I have a friend in San Francisco who says that, after those days when she's cursed people in traffic and been snotty to the poor, Jesus must need a drink. In exasperation Jesus catches hold of Peter and says, "How little faith you have." He catches hold of him, remember; he certainly doesn't let him drown.

By the time Peter names Jesus as the Christ, he's had these experiences. He's wandered with this guy, he's watched him, listened, and walked, for a little while, on the water. Many events have taken place before he gets to the time and the place where he can say, "I know who you are." Naming the Christ in our lives doesn't happen in an instant. It happens over time. It happens when we witness new life unfolding, and sense new possibility. It happens when we experience what Simone Weil called "an impulse of an essentially and manifestly different order."[2]

Faith is not about belief in something irrational or a blind connection to something unreal. It's about an accumulation of events and experiences of a different order. It's about seeing five thousand fed, walking on water, and traveling around with a person who always catches you in the waves. It's about hearing a voice so unimaginably tender you cannot resist its call. And then, you can finally allow yourself to be fully vulnerable to that person, to risk transformation.

There is a postscript to the story of Peter. It's found at the end of John's Gospel. Jesus has died on the cross. His disciples have fled. Peter has gone back to fishing. And then this sweet scene: The fishing has been bad; they've been up all night. A man appears on the beach and tells them where to throw their nets. The nets come up full of fish. The disciple whom Jesus loves points to the man on the beach and says, "It is the Lord." And Peter, our beloved Peter, leaps into the water and swims to shore.

This seems to me the fitting end to this part of the story. Once we have begun to know this life of faith, this journey with this luminous person, we can begin to integrate our experiences with him into our lives. Our faith is not only in the events of a different order, but, as Esther de Waal says, we "let the mundane become the edge of glory."[3] We begin to live in and with the Christ. Peter has more in store for his life, we know, but at this point, he is merely joyful. He doesn't walk on the water, he swims in it. He sees his Lord. And the story isn't over after all.

Nora Gallagher is author of Things Seen and Unseen: A Year Lived in Faith. *She lives in Santa Barbara, California.*

---

2. "Spiritual Autobiography," in *Waiting for God* (New York: Harper & Row, 1951), 63.

3. Esther de Waal, "The Extraordinary in the Ordinary," *Weavings* (May/June 1987), 15.

TERESA OF AVILA

The "Infant"

Matthew 11:25-30

Philip Culbertson

UNTIL RECENTLY, I was pretty sure that Teresa of Avila was another of those medieval saints whose overactive spiritual imaginations were masked by singularly boring lives, preserved in a series of sanitized narratives designed to make me feel guilty about my shortcomings in prayer. My initial impressions were not much alleviated when I opened Teresa's autobiography and read that, as a small child, her favorite pasttime was to take her brother out to the back paddock for a game of "nuns in the hermitage."[1] But gradually an altogether different impression emerged. And the longer I read, the more clear was the connection between the life of Teresa and the passage from Matthew about the wise and the infants, though the connection is more complicated than it might appear. In the Greek version of Matthew, the word translated into English as "infant" is *nepios*. It can mean at least four things: 1) *an infant* (but Teresa was a mature adult); 2) *an innocent* (but Teresa wasn't naive, spiritually, politically, or in terms of human nature); 3) *an uneducated person* (but Teresa was unusually well educated for a woman of her time); 4) *a legal minor*—and here a most unusual connection occurs. In the time of Jesus, Jewish law classified legal minors—the opposite of the legally wise and intelligent—as women, children, the blind and deaf, slaves, criminals, and social eccentrics.[2] Matthew 11:25 could as easily mean that God hides things from adult males, which are then revealed to women and children, criminals and social eccentrics.

I'd make a case here for reading Matthew as affirming that there are truths of God that are hidden from men but revealed to women.[3] Such a

---

1. Teresa of Avila, *The Life of St. Teresa of Avila by Herself*, trans. David Lewis (London: Burnes & Oates, 1962), 4.

2. See Maimonides, Yad, Edut 9:1. Erasmus was among the first to insist that these people should also study Scripture, just as men do; see Alison Weber, *Teresa of Avila and the Rhetoric of Femininity* (Princeton: Princeton University Press, 1990), 21.

3. Contra Kramer and Sprenger's 1486 handbook on witchcraft, *Malleus Malleficarum*, which defined the word *femina* as derived from *fe minus*, lacking in faith; see Weber, 20.

reading is confirmed by two important aspects of Teresa of Avila's life: her Jewish background, and the fact that the most powerful male hierarchy of the Church did everything they could to suppress Teresa's work as dangerous, even heretical.

She was born in 1515 in Castille, Spain. Michaelangelo was painting the ceiling of the Sistine Chapel. During her lifetime, in England the Thirty-Nine Articles of Religion were set forth, and France suffered the horrible wars between Catholics and Huguenots, including the St. Bartholomew's Day Massacre of 1572. Most Jews had been expelled from Spain some fifty years earlier, and were living in ghettos elsewhere in Europe, but some had remained in Spain, converting, at least nominally, to Catholicism. These converts were known as *conversos*, or *marranos*.[4] Among them were the grandparents of Teresa. Many who now study her writings believe she was deeply influenced by that Jewish heritage, kept alive inside her family by home rituals, prayers, and stories. In *The Interior Castle,* she compares the human soul to a silkworm that spins itself into a cocoon and then emerges into a new state of freedom and beauty as a butterfly.[5] This image appears two hundred years before Teresa in a famous Jewish mystical text called *The Zohar.*[6]

A myth has grown up around Teresa that she was a simple woman with a transparent agenda: the edification of the soul and the promotion of a discalced community life. Again the connection with Matthew is complicated, for Teresa was not an infant in educational terms. Her father taught her to read and write and educated her on Cicero and Seneca and Boethius[7]; she attributed much of her spiritual formation to her own personal reading, citing in particular the Letters of St. Jerome, Gregory the Great's *Moralia,* De Osuna's *Third Alphabet,* and St. Augustine's *Confessions.*[8] She wrote books—often reluctantly, insisting that she would rather be spinning—but we aren't even sure how many, for the Spanish Inquisition tried to destroy them almost as fast as she

---

4. See Rowan Williams, *Teresa of Avila* (London: Geoffrey Chapman, 1991), p. 13. On Teresa's Jewish identity, see 34–38.

5. Teresa of Avila, *The Interior Castle,* trans. Kieran Kavanaugh and Otilio Rodroguez (New York: Paulist Press, 1979), 91–94.

6. See Weber, p. 110, and Catherine Swietlicki, *Spanish Christian Cabala: The Works of Luis de León, Santa Teresa de Jesús, and San Juan de la Cruz* (Columbia: University of Missouri Press, 1986), 44–51, 156.

7. Vita Sackville-West, *The Eagle and the Dove: A Study in Contrasts, St. Teresa of Avila and St. Therese of Lisieux* (London: Michael Joseph, 1943), 19–20.

8. *Interior Castle,* 8–9, 50.

could write them.[9] She valued the human intellect highly, insisting that the highest forms of prayer could not be reached without using it. She believed it more important that one's spiritual director be educated than spiritual.[10]

Teresa writes with a sense of charm, and a witty tinge of irony. Complaining to God in prayer about her sufferings and trials, she heard the Lord telling her, "Teresa, that's how I treat my friends!" to emphasize the purifying quality of suffering. Teresa, who knew that already, answered, "Well, that's why you have so few of them!"[11]

She is frequently grumpy, has poor health and headaches, remembers only snippets of the biblical passages she wants to cite, has to stop and cry every once in a while when she thinks about her sisters, forgets what she was talking about, digresses wildly, and can't always remember why she's writing.[12] But medievalist Alison Weber believes much of this is what she calls "The Rhetoric of Female Humility," a clever strategy women mystics adopted to make themselves safe from the male hierarchy of the Church.[13] She characterizes Teresa as defensive, affiliative, and subversive, all at the same time. The male hierarchy could tolerate Teresa's political activism, community organization, and rebellious feminism only because she maintained a persona of groveling female humility and obedience. Even after her death, they found her threatening. They were anxious to describe her as a "virile woman" or a "manly soul." In one of the most famous portraits of her, Elijah and Elisha float above her head on a cloud, holding a banner reading "Our little sister does not have breasts."[14]

The *Oxford Dictionary of the Christian Church* claims that Teresa was the first spiritual writer to note how many different forms of prayer exist. The male-denominated prayer disciplines of her time insisted that oral prayer—the repetition of familiar words—was more important than mental prayer, or praying with a sense of interior meaning, and that prayer was an accomplishable task by which one moved progressively up an ever-increasing ladder of piety toward union with a distant God. Teresa incurred the wrath of her superiors by insisting that mental prayer was a

---

9. The directors of the Inquisition called her commentary on the Song of Songs both "too hyperbolic" and "too literal," apparently failing to notice the contradiction; see Weber, 119.

10. *Interior Castle*, 155, and *Life*, 89. She also said that some spiritual directors will "suck your brains out"; see Weber, 152.

11. Kieran Kavanaugh, "Introduction," *Interior Castle*, xvii.

12. *Interior Castle*, 51, 57, 64, 71.

13. Weber, 14–15.

14. Weber, 17-18.

far more formative activity than oral prayer. Her famous image of the presence of God is not a task-oriented ladder, but a labyrinthine castle deep inside the soul, in which, in prayer, one wandered from one room to the next. Her classic text, known as *The Dwelling Places* or *The Interior Castle*, describes the pilgrim's journey through seven rooms inside that castle, but also asserts that there are many more rooms inside the structure of the soul, for rooms stand off rooms stand off rooms.[15] For Teresa, there is no one form or prayer or one state of being in God's presence that is always right for every person. Prayer is person-specific and context-variable—to stretch us, but always also to meet our needs and abilities in the present.

The one form of mysticism of which she was deeply suspicious was a life of passive contemplation. She describes such detached mystics as "prayer junkies."[16] Emptying ourselves of possessions, pride, and what St. Francis would call "the purse of our own opinions" does not mean that the spiritual task has been accomplished. We must even let go of everything that makes us feel good about our personal faith. Such disciplines, which she called the "evangelical poverty of spirit,"[17] are merely preparatory. Our true spiritual growth can be measured only by our visible works among the people with whom we live. The mystic knows we can never really tell how much we love God, for much of how we image God is a projection of our personal need. We can, however, quite visibly measure how much we love our neighbors by the way we respond to their needs.[18] She spurns Mary, who sat at the feet of Jesus to learn, observing that if everyone were a Mary, no one would have anything to eat because no one would be in the kitchen like Martha.[19] The truly spiritual person has reached a balance between Mary and Martha, busy in the world, yet checking in with God often in order to pray and to listen. Teresa believed that we should serve every person, every neighbor, for God can be found in every person. The Church told her she was wrong; God was found only in people who lead exemplary Christian lives. She decided to stand her ground anyway.[20]

And so in her quiet, charming, ever-determined way, this little old woman took on the Church hierarchy and won. Vita Sackville-West, in a biography of Teresa, described her at the height of her power:

---

15. For a summary of the castle's structure, see *Interior Castle*, 21ff. and 196; for the contrast between male paradigms and female paradigms, see 42.

16. *Interior Castle*, 83.

17. *Interior Castle*, 11.

18. *Interior Castle*, 100. Compare James 2:26: "Faith without works is dead."

19. *Interior Castle*, 192.

20. *Interior Castle*, 7.

She was stout . . . her speech had become indistinct, and she walked leaning always on the crooked ebony staff her brother had brought back from the Indies. Her skin was "the color of earth"; her teeth black with decay; and stiff hairs sprouted from the moles which had once been thought to add charm to her face. Her left arm, which the Devil had broken by throwing her down a flight of stairs one Christmas-eve . . . was almost useless . . . she was quite unable to dress or undress herself or even to adjust her veil.[21]

This little old lady wrote, echoing Matthew 11:25, "Learned and wise men know about these things very well, but [it is necessary to spell everything out] for our womanly dullness of mind."[22] Ironically, the same reference to Matthew backgrounds a report by members of the Inquisition that her writings should be destroyed. They wrote:

> For even though the learned men (whom she consulted and obeyed) may know more about faith and Scripture and the general rules of prayer and contemplation . . . it may well be and often is that a woman knows more with the favor of God and with practice and experience than a speculative, dry, undevout theologian . . . Nevertheless, it is unwise for these books to circulate in the vernacular among men and women.[23]

But circulate they did, and today this *nepios*, this infant, is celebrated by the wise and learned as a Doctor of the Church and as one of the most insightful scribes of the spiritual life that the Church has ever produced.

Of a God who walks amongst the pots and pans,[24] we ask three simple things. Teach us, like Teresa of Avila, to lead a life of prayer and obedience that demonstrates your love to others, yet confirms our sense of self-worth. Teach us the humility that meets others' needs, yet confirms that we survive by both your grace and a healthy dose of intelligent cleverness. Like Teresa, may we spend our days, in this life and the world to come, publicly undermining the pettiness of the Church, and privately wandering the interior castle where we may rejoice in erotic union with you.

Philip Culbertson is Director of Pastoral Studies in the Auckland Consortium for Theological Education, University of Auckland, New Zealand.

---

21. Sackville-West, 89.

22. *Interior Castle*, 41; see also 37, 39, 81.

23. Weber, 162.

24. *The Complete Works of Saint Teresa of Jesus*. Trans. by E. Allison Peers. 3 vols. (London: Sheed and Ward, 1944–46), III.22.

EDWARD BOUVERIE PUSEY

Scribes Trained for the Kingdom

Matthew 13:52-53
Roger Alling

IN EUCHARISTIC SERVICES, after the gospel is read, the Deacon raises the book and says: "The gospel of the Lord." The people respond, "Praise to you, Lord Christ." Once a young priest was preaching at a service where the Bishop was presiding. Unfortunately, the sermon had been hastily prepared and wasn't very good. Finishing the sermon, looking for some concluding sentence, the priest loudly proclaimed: "This is the gospel of the Lord." In an audible stage whisper, the Bishop responded: "I seriously doubt it!"

What did the Bishop hear that prompted this remark? *A discrepancy between God's Word in the gospel and the words about the gospel in the priest's sermon.* Perhaps the Bishop thought this particular scribe needed more training before he would be able to bring out, in the pulpit, treasures old and new.

Scribes trained for the Kingdom of Heaven—able to bring out veritable treasures! Is this what Jesus wanted for his disciples? Is such training what the Pharisees rejected? Did that rejection prompt the telling of these parables? Is there training Jesus wants us to undertake in preparation for preaching the gospel? If this is a word of God to us, it is a challenge and a promise: a challenge to be better scribes; a promise that we will have treasures, old and new, to share.

Today we commemorate Edward Bouverie Pusey. He was a scribe fitly trained for the Kingdom of Heaven, one who brought out old and new treasures. Think for a moment of nineteenth-century England, the context of Pusey's life. The Industrial Revolution was under way. Workers were on the move from the countryside into the cities, often living in squalid surroundings. The Church was not following these people adequately as they made this transition. Church leaders understood that change and renewal were necessary. The renewal took two forms. The evangelical renewal focused on foreign missions to the far reaches of the British Empire. The Oxford movement, in its inception, stayed closer home. Members concentrated their work on the newly populated inner cities of industrial England, attempting to bring the gospel and the Church to the cities' new residents. These men were also responsible for the rediscovery of Catholic elements in church life and liturgy that had fallen into disuse in English churches. This movement, centered in Oxford university life, was led by Edward Pusey, John Keble, and John Henry Newman.

Today the Oxford movement is most remembered for its innovations in liturgy and ceremonial ornamentation. The movement, however, was concerned with weightier matters. Of great concern to these reformers was reemphasis on Church teaching and doctrine: the Real Presence of Christ in the Eucharist, the importance of baptism, sacramental penance, and the renewal of monasteries and the religious life.

Edward Pusey was an agent of change in the Church of England. No change is effected without cost, and there were costs for Pusey. Pusey was a preacher. Some of the changes he proposed for the Church were expressed in university sermons. Some of these "university sermons" got him into trouble with his superiors, and he was prohibited from preaching for two years. He had other troubles as well. A serious crisis loomed when John Henry Newman left Anglicanism and joined the Roman Catholic Church. Was this to be the beginning of large-scale defections of others in the Oxford movement? Fortunately, Pusey stood fast for reforms within Anglicanism, and kept other leaders from following Newman's move. To his credit, Pusey maintained an irenic spirit with Newman and others throughout the controversy. Pusey continued his work of reform and preaching throughout his life. His last ministry, after the death of his wife, involved substantial aid for the founding of Anglican religious orders.

Jesus' promise to the trained scribes was preceded by parables. Perhaps their teaching will contribute to our training as scribes for God—parables of the treasure in the field, and the gem merchant. Both have elements of surprise that lead to new challenges and new opportunities

A man wanders aimlessly, stubs his toe on a box, digs around it with his walking stick, and discovers a fortune hidden ages ago by someone long dead. Every day a merchant buys and sells gems of modest value. It is all very routine, but it puts bread on the table. Then one day in a pawnshop he spies *the pearl!* Both of these characters are stopped in their tracks. *Wow! What now?* The *Wow!* is the surprise. The *What now?* is the recognition that normal daily living is interrupted: *Bet the ranch! Go for broke! Sell all to buy the field! Get the gem!*

Is it not true that in our work sometimes we stub our toes and stumble into hidden treasure? Is it not true that at other times we only come across the treasure after searching in all the gem stores and pawnshops of this world? What matters is not how we come upon the treasure, but what we do when we have it. The *Wow!* is fine, but the *What now?* is vital! The trained scribe will be brought to a halt, set other things aside, do what needs to be done to own the treasure. Then we will have something to share, treasures new and old to bring to our people for their good and for the good of the world.

When Edward Pusey discovered treasures, he interrupted his life and brought them out to share with others. We are among the beneficiaries of his ministry, for his work added to the depth and richness of our Anglican tradition. I am particularly grateful to him because his work came into focus for me during my last two seminary years.

After Pusey's death a beautiful center for religious studies was built in Oxford near the St. Giles memorial to Cranmer and Ridley. Pusey House has a fine library and a large chapel. The clergy staff there offer chaplaincy services to Oxford students and city residents. On Sunday mornings during term, a splendid Eucharist is celebrated, incorporating all those external features the Tractarians reintroduced to Anglicanism. But it is never just a celebration of beautiful old things. The center of the services is the sermon. Preachers of renown from the United Kingdom and around the world are invited to preach at these special services, and the sermons there are among the best I have ever heard.

I doubt Pusey could have known the effect his reforms would have in the Anglican Communion. But then, who of us knows what impact we may have as we bring out new treasures to add to the rich ones we have already received?

Roger Alling is co-editor of this volume.

MARTIN LUTHER KING JR.

Living in Hope

Romans 8:22-25
Eddie Blue

WE HAVE COME HERE to do something radically Christian. We have abandoned the traditional day for celebrating Dr. King's life and ministry, his birthday, January fifteenth, and chosen to celebrate on the day of his assassination. Not that we take any pleasure in recalling this event, but Christians understand death to be not a closing of life but an entry into larger life. King's association with the world he helped to shape may have ended, but his life with God has been expanded and enriched. Today we testify to a living hope that we share and are called to proclaim. I take as my text these words from the eighth chapter of Romans:

We know that the whole creation has been groaning in labor pains until now; and not only the creation, but we ourselves, who have the first fruits of the Spirit, groan inwardly while we wait for adoption, the redemption of our bodies. For in hope we were saved. Now hope that is seen is not hope. For who hopes for what is seen? But if we hope for what we do not see, we wait for it with patience.

Paul is writing to members of a church. We can imagine what they are like: fractious and contentious, mean-spirited and cruel, faithful and loving, gentle and kind, generous and noble. They live under persecution. Many in the Roman Empire consider them immoral, threats to good order. Some Christians begin to wonder why they who love the Lord live in such anguish. Had they known the song they might have sung,

They say we are the Lord's Children and I don't say that ain't true,
But if we are the Lord's children, why do they treat me like they do?[1]

So Paul writes to remind and assure them of their calling and their hope. They have been called by the Spirit to be children of God, and their hope is in Jesus. Paul promises that those who die in him will surely rise with him. The Church has already had a foretaste, an appetizer, of the glory of God. Their hope is that the promise will be fulfilled—a glory that will make suffering pale in significance. They must live in hope. Dr. King carried this Spirit of Hope to Memphis.

Often when people of my generation discuss the sixties a wistful glow comes over their faces. It is as if they were transported to another place and time. For just a second, they're remembering all the dope they smoked, the way they wore their hair, how they talked about peace and love or shouted "Off the pigs!" You sense a longing beyond nostalgia, a desire to live those days again. I am not as sanguine about those times. The sixties were a time of great social transformation but not all of it was good. True, one can point to events in those days as the beginning of improvement in the plight of minorities and women. But one can also point to the beginning of the end of civility and chastity, the collapse of moral authority and honor.

I was happy during those times. I had given little thought to the world around me. As I know now, part of the reason is that my mother, like

---

1. James Cone, *The Spirituals and the Blues* (Maryknoll, N.Y.: Orbis Books, 1973, 1991), 121.

many black parents of the day, took pains to protect my family from the ravages of racism. White people existed in a faraway place, in history books, on TV. But one cannot stay protected forever. After walking with three friends to one part of the city, I discovered there were places you couldn't go if you were black. One of my friends got punched in the face. We were chased out of the neighborhood just because they didn't want people like us there.

A pall hovered over our existence as black people. On the one hand, we were in the Land of Opportunity. We had been taught that everything was possible for us. There was no mountain too high to climb, no job we could not enter, no office to which we could not aspire. On the other hand, there was this niggling voice whispering: "This is not for you . . . you're not wanted here . . . you are doomed to fail . . . it will be ever thus!" It was the voice of American culture speaking to us plainly, constantly, inexorably.

Swiftly, things began to change. We moved from strength to strength. *Brown vs. The Board of Education* forced school integration. Sit-ins by black students began all over the South as a challenge to Jim Crow. Montgomery, Selma, and Birmingham became key scenes in the struggle for equality. And Martin Luther King Jr. emerged from the obscurity of Dexter Avenue Baptist Church to become the leader of a movement.

Perhaps the high point of his life as head of the movement was his "I Have a Dream" speech, spoken during the March on Washington. King called America to live up to the promises made to its people and trumpeted around the world. He recalled to all who would hear that America had said, "All men are created equal." And he called upon America to live out this creed, painting a picture of what things could be like someday. We could live in harmony, we could walk together as brothers and sisters, we could be one nation. His speech called us to live in hope. It was so thrilling that we dared to hope. Martin was like one of the old slave preachers, gathering his flock at night in the shadow of the big house, preaching: "You are not slaves, you are not niggers, you are free!"

A lot had changed by the time King came to Memphis. He was a Nobel laureate. The Voting Rights Act and Civil Rights Act had been passed. It seemed as though the necessary work of the movement had been done. King had publicly opposed the Black Power Movement. The whole nation had seen the Watts section of Los Angeles erupt in flames. King came to Memphis with diminished influence in both white and black America because he was one of the first national leaders to oppose the Vietnam War. No one believed that the Civil Rights Movement should shift its focus from further gains. We wanted one message, "Freedom Now," and we didn't want it diluted by anti-war activity. Black people are patriots.

We love this country. The blood, backs, and bones of our ancestors built this country, so we love it. One way that we could express our love for country and claim our place in it was through military service. For Dr. King to suggest that this war was wrong was to call into question our patriotism and our honor.

Dr. King's genius, however, was that he saw the connection between oppression and racism at home and war abroad. He saw no moral difference between segregated housing in America and bombing villages in Vietnam. (We must acknowledge today that there is no moral disconnect between the United States' abuse of Indian rights, racial profiling, bombing villages in Kosovo, starving the people of Iraq, and a legal system that seems to operate only for the rich and powerful. There can be no peace without justice.)

Dr. King came to Memphis. Why? Thirteen hundred sanitation workers knew nothing but work—ten hours a day, six days a week. In rain, sleet, snow, and in the oppressive heat of summer they worked. Without bathroom breaks or lunch breaks they worked. They had low pay, no benefits, no way to air their grievances or establish work rules.

Under the leadership of O.T. Jones they organized into a union. They sought a meeting with the mayor, who declared he would meet with any individual but not with a group. They decided to strike. The sanitation workers could have carried signs that said, "Higher Wages" or "More Benefits." Instead they carried placards or wore sandwich boards reading, "I Am a Man." "I am a man," said, "I am a human being. I must be taken seriously." It said, "You may call me a 'walking buzzard,' but I am a person. You must reckon with me." It said to the workers themselves, "We are men, and men take care of their families. Men feed and clothe and house their wives and children."

The strike was protracted. After several weeks, even with garbage piling up and no end to the strike in sight, the interest of the strikers and the public began to wane. Dr. Benjamin Hooks, then a local magistrate and later president of the NAACP, asked King to come to Memphis. He was reluctant at first. He had intended to go to Africa to support liberation movements there, but he came to realize that the work in Memphis spoke to what he believed and lived for.

He came in mid-February and tried to mediate a meeting with the mayor and the strikers, but failed. He organized marches, which were well attended but marred by violence. Some young men separated themselves from the march and went about smashing windows. King left Memphis after two weeks, intending to return in March. A massive snowstorm delayed his return until April. He delivered his last speech on April 3, 1968.

By his standards, it was not a great speech. Well thought out, but given extemporaneously, it lacked the polish of others. He urged the people to remain united, to ask not "What is going to happen to me if I support this strike?" but "What will happen to the sanitation workers if I don't?" He made suggestions about how the community could use its economic clout collectively to move the city toward resolution of the strike. He held firm in his conviction that non-violent action would win the day.

King recalled all that he had witnessed in the struggle for freedom and spoke of how glad he was to be alive to see what was happening in the country and the world. Finally, he talked about the threats made against his life:

> Well, I don't know what will happen now. We've got some difficult days ahead. But it doesn't matter with me now. Because I've been to the mountaintop. And I don't mind. Like anybody, I would like to live a long life. Longevity has its place. But I'm not concerned about that now. I just want to do God's will. And He's allowed me to go up to the mountain. And I've looked over. And I've seen the Promised Land. I may not get there with you but I want you to know tonight, that we, as a people, will get to the promised land. And I'm happy tonight. I'm not worried about anything. I'm not fearing any man. Mine eyes have seen the glory of the coming of the Lord.[2]

The next day he was dead, felled by an assassin's bullet. Blacks in cities all over America, acting against all that he had lived and died for, vented their rage and anguish by rioting. National Guards and federal troops quelled the rioting. President Johnson sent Attorney General Ramsay Clark to mediate the strike in Memphis. Less than three weeks after King's death, the strike was settled.

It would be easy to say that his influence ended with his death, but hope is stronger than death. Hope means hanging on to a vision than is greater than what you can ask for or imagine. Hope means understanding that there is glory still to be revealed. Being a Christian means living in hope.

Another, more recent image has emerged from Memphis, an image of hope growing out of horrible violence. A firefighter killed his wife, set fire to his garage, and called in the alarm. As the fire trucks arrived, he shot and killed a fireman and a police officer. A picture was taken in the aftermath of the deranged killer's apprehension. It shows four firemen: two

---

2. Martin Luther King Jr., "I See the Promised Land," in *A Testament of Hope: The Essential Writings and Speeches of Martin Luther King Jr.*, ed. James M. Washington (New York: Harper Collins, 1986), 286.

white, two black. They are dressed in their insulated overalls, but they have taken off their helmets and coats. They are doing what human beings have always done to bring one another solace and comfort; they are hugging one another. Thirty-two years ago I could not have imagined men of different races working together, living together, bearing one another's burdens in Memphis. But hope is greater than our imagination. Hope can propel us into a bright future. Hope is stronger than death. Live in hope.

Eddie Blue is Rector of the Church of the Holy Trinity,
Baltimore, Maryland.

SAINT MICHAEL AND ALL ANGELS
THE CELEBRATION OF A NEW MINISTRY

Angelic Failure, Angelic Joy

2 Corinthians 4
Leander S. Harding

WHEN I WAS in seminary and graduate school, voices in the Church urged us to downplay the miraculous, the supernatural, the otherworldly. If we wanted to reach contemporary people, we were told, we should stress "this-worldly" aspects of the faith. The Church listened to this counsel. We have gained much from a renewed emphasis on practical love of the neighbor. But as we enter the twenty-first century, the mysterious, the miraculous, the supernatural—elements of the life of faith about which we were almost embarrassed—are just the things in which people are most interested. Twenty years ago talk about angels would have been dismissed as antiquated and irrelevant. Now people in this country long to be "touched by an angel." What, I wonder, do angels themselves think of this new-found attention? What would they say about it? If you will allow an exercise of imagination, I believe they would say something like this:

We are spirits who dwell continually in the presence of God, ordained to bring you messages of his love and tokens of his healing. We are meant to guard you, keep you from evil influence, and call you to justice, mercy, and righteousness, to remind you of the life eternal and give you hope in the face of death, to intimate to you the glory of the worship in heaven and encourage you to join with us as you worship here on earth. Long ago we found out we could not really do what God had ordained for us. We found that human beings after the Fall (that is, after humans forgot who God is, and what it means to be human—having a heart right toward God and right toward brothers and sisters) have an allergy to the things of God. A full-fledged angelic manifestation leaves them terrified and doubting their senses. (We get very weary of saying, "Fear not.") Even worse, men and women who receive a message at the hands of an angel believe and obey because they are impressed or frightened. This is a problem because we are under strict instructions to present our message of God's freely given love in such a way that the person receiving the message can choose to accept it or not. This means we often have to operate at low candlepower. It is very hard to get it right. We end up being either too overwhelming, or too subtle to be noticed. The problems go on and on, for when people do hear the message, they ignore it as being from and for angels, not for mere mortals. Even worse, they sometimes think they should try to become angels. But our message is not that men and women should become angelic but that they should become more fully human. In any case, it is as unnatural and impossible for human beings to become angels as it is for cats to become dogs. So we end up with results that betray our mission and heart's desire to serve the loving purposes of God. We were at the end of our rope with all this until he decided to become one with you so that you could become one with him.

The baby in the manger and later the man on the cross bring you to your knees without scaring you out of your wits. You can even accept his Resurrection, because he has shown you his hands and his side. You cannot shrug off the message and the challenge of a life of love as unrealistic because you know he was tempted in every way as you are and yet did not sin. The best doctor is one who knows exactly where and how it hurts. The best helper is one who walks beside you and knows what your shoes feel like. He can help you in ways we never could. Now you have a healer, helper, guide, and defender who will be with you always, even to the end of the age. If he is in you and you are in him, as he is, so you shall be. Your destiny is to be higher than we are, and we will sing hosannas at your transfiguration and minister to you in eternity.

He has come, has done, and does what we were under sacred obligation to do, wanted to do, and could not do. Until he appeared, our ordination was an ordination to failure. In redeeming you, he has redeemed us. Now we have a ministry we can do and gladly do—point to him.

So, we find ourselves at this Celebration of New Ministry on the Feast of Michael and All Angels. As we come to ask God's blessing on priest and people, who commit themselves to one another and recommit themselves to God, entering a new chapter of parish life together, the angels' song is in the air. What they say to us is pertinent for the ministry of priest and people. Mortals and angels occupy different orders in God's creation and should not be confused, but the ministry of the priest shares this with the ministry of the angels: it is an ordination to failure.

You have allowed me to give voice to the angels tonight, allow me now to give voice to the priesthood. The priestly life forces us to say: *I have been ordained to pray without ceasing and to so dwell in the presence of God that I might continuously and unfailingly bring you messages of his love and tokens of his healing. I am ordained to guard the souls of those entrusted to my care, to guard the spirit (the Book of Revelation calls it the angel) of this congregation, to keep you individually and collectively from evil influence. I am to order our worship so that it intimates the glory of the worship in heaven. I am ordained to call you to justice, mercy, and righteousness, to call you to repentance, and to pronounce absolution and blessing. I am to remind you of the life eternal and give you hope in the face of death.*

I cannot do any of this. It is not humanly possible because of my frailty and inadequacy to the task, and because of that resistance to the things of God that we all share. I can only fail to do that which I have been ordained to do, but I have promised, taken a sacred oath, never to stop trying. The more faithful and diligent the attempt, the deeper I must go into my poverty as a person, and a priest, the more I must taste of the mystery of that failure I share with the angels—to be obligated to bring a message, to want above all else to bring it, and to be completely inadequate to the task until he shall appear. So priesthood bids me taste the mystery of angelic failure and bids me die. And here begins to appear a portion of that mystery into which angels long to look: The more I die, the more I am able to point to him. And this is different from the ministry of angels: The more I die, the more he makes his appeal through me. The more I die, as St. Paul says, the more I carry about in my body the death of Christ, that the life of Christ might be made known in me as well. The more I die, the more he is present to his people through my ministry, the more effective the sacramental sign of priesthood is in me, and the more I begin to know the mystery of the joy angels have in seeing him appear and touch, redeem, and transfigure people with the eternal Word of God's Love.

It is customary at times like this to give a charge to priest and people alike. To your priest I say: Do not fear failure. Angelic failure is the secret of your priesthood. May you plumb this secret and know the sadness and frustration of the angels that you may know their joy. May it be given to you here: by your weakness and utter dependence on him, the Word of God's Love is made present, and the angels' song of praise rises in your heart as you see him do what you cannot.

To this people, this parish, I say: Here is a gifted, competent, personable man. He can do many things well. He can't do everything equally well. (He is a package deal like all the rest of us.) God means to use his gifts and talents, along with yours, to be a blessing in this place. But there is a further blessing to be had, one threatened with eclipse in our Church, one I challenge a Catholic parish to seek—the blessing God intends for his Church through the sacramental sign of the priesthood. For this to come to pass you must allow your priest to be weak, broken-hearted, poor. You must allow him to be a disappointment and a failure. You must allow him to be empty-handed, to have nothing of his own and thereby to allow him more and more by his own weakness, by his own dying, by his own utter dependence on God, to bring you the One who alone is able to save, redeem, and transfigure us, Jesus Christ Our Lord, to whom be the honor and the glory now and forever.

Leander S. Harding is Rector of St. John's Church,
Stamford, Connecticut.

A Sermon Preached at the Installation of the Rev. Dr. Charles Miller as Sixth Rector of the Church of the Transfiguration, New York City.

THE BAPTISM OF OUR LORD

Claiming Our Calling

Mark 1:7-11
Jennifer Phillips

I STRAP ON SCUBA gear and tumble backward into clear Caribbean Sea on what is, perhaps, my tenth dive after certification. Around me, in explosions of bubbles, other bulky bodies cannonade through the bright skin of the water, righting themselves and finning downward toward the reef. The photographers come last, requiring hands from the boat to pass down their cameras in bubble housings, their lights on folding steel arms, their extra lenses and accessory bags. The non-photographers give them a wide berth, envious of the mysterious world they capture with delicate lenses, disdainful of their habits of intruding upon fragile coral with careless fins, bruising and crushing the life of the reef outside their viewfinders.

I clear my ears and let myself settle slowly down through changing layers of blue beside the coral wall: thirty feet, fifty . . . pausing to watch tiny shrimp and shy fish in the crevices . . . through seventy and ninety feet, finally hovering just above a plain of sand at a hundred feet down, where the weight of the water gives palpable compression to every inch of my body, and the light is a dim indigo. Thousands of sand eels no bigger than pencils are swaying from their burrows in the ocean floor like a miniature field of umbrella handles with eyes. The silence, too, feels like a weight: thick and substantial, broken only by the gurgles and whistles of my breathing and the regulator's mechanical response.

Suddenly there's a movement in my peripheral vision and a *THUMP* to the side of my head. The landscape disappears in a flash of bubbles and a blur. I inhale a nose-full of saltwater. A careening photographer has descended on top of me, anxious for a shot of sand eels. He kicks off my mask without even noticing me. Every impulse in my body screams: "Kick for the surface!" Panic! The water burns my nose and throat; I want to cough. It is possible to make a free ascent from one hundred feet. It is also possible to get the bends doing so, as nitrogen bubbles from the blood into the joints, without time to be cleared from the body as you go up.

One part of my brain says clearly, "Your regulator is still in your mouth; you can breathe. You need not drown, even if you feel like you surely will. Breathe through your mouth. Locate the mask." And so, as every new diver is trained to do, I breathe, resist the cough reflex, and begin to feel around on the sand for my lost mask. My heart is pounding in my ears. Gradually I realize I am not quite blind. My surroundings are a dim blur, but I can pick out the dark edge of the wall against the lighter sand. Turning slowly, I see a beige smear against the uniform shading of the sea floor. I reach down and feel rubber. Painstakingly, I feel for the strap and the nose, get the mask right side up, clamp it against my face, pull the strap over, and blow out my nose. Air displaces the water. Suddenly, through stinging eyes, I can see. And now I'm really, really mad at the jerk who kicked me and never even stopped to notice.

This memory came to me recently in meditating on vocation. How is it that we seek and discover our vocations as God's people? How do we find our way? How do we know what God has in mind for us? Can we know at all? How can we tell if we have chosen well? How can we cope with panic at the overwhelming scope of life directions and choices? As a child, I imagined Jesus rising up from the waters of baptism with calm confidence, striding into ministry, never looking back, never doubting his path. In the middle of my life now, I envision him dripping, breathless, expectant, his own heart torn open like the heavens by this sudden awareness of God's delight and favor. Then I see him overwhelmed at the open possibilities before him, at the largeness of the world and its trouble, at the desperation of human beings around him, flocking to John, with the burden of their sin heavy around their necks. I read and hear of Jesus driven into the desert by Satan straightaway, finding himself pushed and pulled, knowing that he can never go back to the old life, the old security, that everything has irrevocably changed, that forward is the only way to go—into the future, the unknown imperative of God. There he was, I suspect: hoping, expecting, shaken, yearning, resolute, wondering, perhaps even panic-stricken!

When panic strikes in the life of faith, that impulse to escape, even knowing there is no life to be had elsewhere, we are summoned back to the discipline of our formation. Back to steady prayer, by which the oxygen of God's presence sustains and enters us, and the waste of our lives is exhaled and carried away; back to the Sacraments, which nourish and cleanse us; back to the community, which in its broken, inept, yet grace-filled way bears us along when we cannot find our own way; back to the constancy of service among those whose plight is more pressing than our own; and back to the mystery of our lives hid with God and wrapped in God's great love. Called always into change and the future through the covenant of our baptism.

You will remember how the disciples went running back to Jesus breathless with their experience of ineptitude and failure when they met up with demons too big for them as they ventured out alone. "This kind," Jesus tells them patiently, "can be cast out only by fasting and by prayer."

"So you have a decision in front of you," said a wise friend to me once. "Consider for a moment that this which seems so weighty may not matter in quite the way you think. Consider that you may be free to choose trusting in God's great delight in you, God's great desire for you, God's great power to bless your choice, and you in the choosing. Now, talk to me about each of your options. Let's listen for where the energy is, where the life is for you in them; and I will tell you what I hear."

Sometimes decisions about God's calling can be worked out rationally by toting up the pros and cons, by holding our choices up to the yardstick of the gospel; at other times we must allow them to well up from hidden places out of another kind of wisdom, informed by the Spirit of God that is in us.

At some moments, God's calling is like a boat into which we step, and are carried to an entirely unprecedented shore. A whole life direction is shaped in the step of a single moment, and we know it as we step. At other times, we tread along a familiar path step by step, uphill and down, and God's small still voice whispers, "Yes, this way, this way." Sometimes we wander long distances, uncertain of our course, very cross with God for having stayed behind while we went on into danger. And then, perhaps a long while later, we consider that perhaps God is looking back over the map of our travels with us, saying, "Yes, in this I called you, and in this; in this you went the other way, but my love prevented you (went before you) and was with you even there."

"Follow your bliss," says popular guru Joseph Campbell. There is both truth and danger there, as a life-charting method. Anglican writer Elizabeth Goudge observes: "To go through the Gospels and note them all is a frightening experience." "Conversion," she says, "is sterile unless one can face and implement the paradox of Christ. He is God and a man on the gallows. His voice is the beauty of the world and the crying of a hungry child. He is peace in our hearts and conviction of sin. He draws us to him with tenderness and then says the most uncomfortable things to us."

"The converted," Goudge adds, "can face a great danger. It is that when the skill of Christ has brought us to him, we forget about his children in concentration about himself. It seems impossible, but we can almost forget the very suffering the thought of which was at one time driving us nearly mad. But Christ won't be concentrated on in this one-sided manner. He is completely identified with all suffering creatures and we have him with them, or not at all. It can come about that some man or woman finds God not by way of a sense of unity with his children but through a journey lonely as that of the Prodigal Son, but I believe that if we go home like the Prodigal Son we must go out again as the Good Samaritan."[1] We are called inevitably forward, into change, toward the suffering world in all its immensity; there is no going back. To step forward may be bliss, but it is also fearful to fall into the hands of the living God!

I recall sitting in a monastery chapel on retreat at prayer. My eyes would not stay closed, but were drawn again and again to the cross where the image of Jesus was haloed by a branch of redbud berries as deeply scarlet as spattered blood against the pale stone wall, the dark wood of the cross, as it were, sprouting into a living, fruit-bearing tree. I saw the baptized Jesus fulfilling his vocation to heal the world oppressed by the devil with a gift of blood and fruitfulness. It is bliss to live close to the heart of God, to feel your heart open to its origins and destiny in love, but it is not necessarily pleasure. It is bliss to surrender yourself into the power of Resurrection. The path we walk to arrive there, however, is the path of change and loss, the valley of the shadow of death. When its fear besets us, behold, God has prepared a table before us, anointed us with oil, gone before us to guide, filled our cup to overflowing, invited us into the eternal courts of light. Come, let us go up!

Jennifer Phillips is Rector of St. Augustine's Church, Kingston, Rhode Island.

---

1. Elizabeth Goudge, *The Joy of the Snow* (New York: Coward, McCann, 1974), 138.

THE ORDINATION OF A DEACON
NATIVITY OF JOHN THE BAPTIST

Bridge Building/Circle Widening

Luke 1:57-80
Katharine Jefferts Schori

WHAT IN THE WORLD does John the Baptist have to do with today's celebration? If John hadn't gone into the baptizing and preaching business, he probably would have been a construction foreman. He builds a road in the desert, starts in on a bridge between the old and the new. He rearranges the walls around Israel to create a new opening into the hearts of people. He's both a demolition expert and a foundation builder; all that business about "repenting" is asking the people of Israel to tear down the false front they've been hiding behind. And the water in the Jordan goes into making a strong concrete foundation.

Maybe John's really an expert remodeler. You see someone in overalls. He never seems to have time to cook a meal. He's not the sort of architect who spends all day in the office. He gets out in the field, puts on a hard hat, and mucks around in the foundation hole. And then his cousin comes along and builds on the foundation that John has been at pains over. But the building doesn't end up being the stone fortress Israel wants. For walls, this home has the open air. There's room for everyone imaginable to come in and take a load off. The food is simple most days, but there's enough and to spare. Potlatch for all comers.

We're here today to give thanks for the older cousin and to bless and name another construction supervisor. Anne already knows something about remodeling, and she's going to get lots more experience. Her job as a deacon is to build bridges—good, strong ones—between communities. She's going to need to learn even more about how to dismantle weak and dangerous ones and build new ones in their places. We're ordaining Anne to build bridges between Lakota and *wasichu* (whites), between those inside the Church and those outside, between the hurting and those who can help healing. We're going to ask her to find those who are searching for God and guide their feet to a solid bridge.

But in another sense, this day is not about Anne, even though she gets a speaking role like John the Baptist. This day is about the bridges that are yet to be built. John helped build the foundation, then got out of the way. This day is about each one of us, and the kinds of bridges we're going to build. What does the bridge from north to south look like? The one from east to west? From a four-directions, sacred-circle way of thinking, to living a cross-shaped life? The open arms of Jesus—on the cross, on Easter morning, healing and feeding and teaching—they are the most profound bridge we know. It's the beginning of a circle, the sacred circle that enfolds all humanity, and all creation.

Anne is called to a difficult work. We're asking her to stand on the edge, between two cultures, so that she can help us all build broader, more inclusive bridges. The *wicasa wakan* (spiritual leader) must stand on the edge of the community, like all prophets. Some days she will find it lonely, but she will also find gifts there on the edge. We'll ask her to challenge us, annoy us, nag us, and invite us into ever-larger circles. Many of us will resist—that's when the prophet has to cry, "Repent" yet again! Her burden, however, is never carried alone. Her role is to remind each of us that we all share in this work. Bridges are not built by individuals—they need enormous crews. Great circles need many hands to stretch around the many nations.

This is a city in desperate need of more bridges. Look at the division between northeast and northwest Portland, or between Burnside and Dunthorpe. Look at the invisibility of neighbors who come from another culture. Consider how seldom the different worshipping congregations in this building join together. Anne is being asked continually to remind us of the people who haven't yet found a bridge, of those outside the circle. Her special concern will be for those who have been pushed off the bridge or shut out of the circle. Her job is to look for them, and remind us to look for them. Sometimes, as Pogo says, they may be us.

The work of a deacon is a lot like John's: make a lot of noise, then get out of the way when people start to listen. That's counter cultural in both Indian and white communities—that's what it means to live on the edge. Deacons have to be annoying, they have to make noise, sometimes they have to stand up and make speeches. That's not always encouraged around the council fire. And getting out of the way so that somebody else's message can be heard does not get big rewards in Anglo culture.

Anne, we're asking you to nag us. Nag us to build broader bridges, to open our circles wider. Nag us to find the bridge between despair and hope. Nag us and challenge us to change the systems of injustice all around us. Encourage us all to put our varied and abundant gifts to work, because every single one of us is needed for this web of living bridges, and indeed, we need all those people who haven't gotten close to a bridge yet.

The architecture of these bridges is *wakan*, holy, mysterious. The possibility has to be there before construction can begin. That vision, that blueprint, that faith has to be held up like a framework on which human beings can begin to make tentative steps. Anne's job is to hold up a blueprint and mobilize the construction crew, to tell the people on each end of the project what the folks on the other end are up to.

In *Indiana Jones and the Last Crusade,* the hero is told he will have to cross a great chasm to reach his goal. There is no obvious bridge—all he can see is empty space. But he's been told that a bridge of light will appear once he commits himself and steps out over that void. He finally rustles up his courage and steps out; the bridge materializes before him. Anne's job is to encourage all of us to tell those stories of possibility, to see ourselves as fellow bridge-makers, willing to risk all in order to reach whoever needs us on the other side, willing to trust God's vision for that bridge.

For years there was a highway ramp on the south side of Seattle that started off into space. I don't know if it's finished yet. Sometimes that happens to us. We may start a bridge from one side, but the time to build the other end hasn't come yet. John's ministry was like that—he preached and baptized and then went to prison and to his death without seeing the whole bridge finished. He had an inkling of what might be coming, some kind of a blueprint, but he never got to see the glory of the Easter bridge. The work of a deacon is like that. It calls for faithfulness, not waiting around for the end results. In the final analysis, we build bridges because that's what was asked from us at baptism. Anne is going to remind us of that.

This Church of ours, this body of Christ is a holy circle. But it's one that can be infinitely larger. Its webs of connection can extend to many more communities. Many more people are crying out to hear and experience the good news we share.

Time to get the crew moving. Time to hold up the blueprint, point to the design of God. Time to see the sacred mirrored in every human being. The call goes out, the whistle blows, the drums are beating, the bells are ringing. It's our watch now. The bridge is a-building!

Katharine Jefferts Schori is the Bishop of Nevada.

This sermon was preached at the ordination to the diaconate of Anne Scissons at the Church of St. Michael and All Angels Church, and the Four Winds Native American Community, Portland, Oregon.

THE ORDINATION OF A BISHOP

Steadfast in Love

John 21:15-17

Fredrica Harris Thompsett

THE ORDINATION of a bishop for the people of God is an exciting undertaking! Look about you . . . A lot is going on! As that great popular theologian of the obvious Yogi Berra once noted, "You can observe a lot by looking!" Your attention may focus on the variety of languages expressed among us, on the wonder, love, and praise of multicultural music, on the words of a medieval mystic, on splashing baptismal waters, on ancient and modern liturgies made new today amid God's people. There is a lot going on! This episcopal ordination follows the radically expansive ministerial mandate of The Book of Common Prayer published in 1979. Bishops are *not* lifted up as ministerial lone rangers! This celebration of a new ministry in episcopal orders is a celebration of *all* baptismal ministries. In this religious family, baptism and episcopal ministry stand side by side, shaping who we are, who we become, and how our diocesan mission as the body of Christ is expressed in the worldwide Church. English Bishop and theologian Stephen Sykes insists: "No one ever gets 'beyond' baptism."[1] If you came here simply to see Bud ordained, you will miss much of this service's intent! This celebration is designed to advance the ministry of us all.

In a consumer culture, however, spectators rule! So today we must resist the temptation to observe as bystanders. Ordinations are not spectator sports, any more than marriages and holy unions are only for the couple seeking the blessing of God and the community, any more than Holy Baptism is a sacrament for private lives, any more than priestly eucharistic actions are complete without the people's great "AMEN!" In Anglican and other traditions, "prayer is responding to God." Our presence and responsiveness are not politely requested, they are essential. Moreover, there are challenges ahead for each of us, challenges about calling and sending, challenges in stories of forgiveness and loyalty, challenges in glimpses of the Holy at work in our midst. Here are

---

1. Stephen Sykes, *Unashamed Anglicanism* (Nashville: Abingdon Press, 1995), 189.

some fortifying provisions for those challenges, drawn from three of my favorite ministerial sponsors: biblical revelation, historical witness, and contemporary theology.

The first place of prominence goes, as it must, to Scripture. The Gospel passage for today is one of astounding clarity and mystery. This text, from the Epilogue of the Gospel of John, begins with an evocative post-Resurrection appearance. It is simply written, marked by great reverence, full of teaching about the Church's mission, and saturated with the palpable presence of divine love. The disciples are gathered by the waterside. The risen Jesus appears and turns a failed fishing expedition into a miraculous catch of fish. Then together they share a lakeside breakfast with provisions they have brought and he has caught. In this post-breakfast challenge the risen Lord calls, forgives, and commissions Peter for future work! Again the call has come to Peter, who has heard the call before, Peter who long ago responded to that first waterside invitation to fish for humanity. This time the summons is to a ministry of reconciliation framed in a direct series of questions, answers, and responses. "Simon, Son of John, do you love me?" "Lord, you know that I love you." "Then feed my sheep." The authoritative commission is repeated again and yet again.

In this dramatic presentation we hear a call of profound simplicity: if you love Jesus, care for others. A lot is going on! In the wonder of our Lord's appearing, forgiveness and reconciliation accurately and baptismally precede new ministries. Peter's threefold professions of loyalty wash away his earlier denials of the Lord. Amid the wonder of this post-Resurrection appearance a call is issued in love, renewed motivation is grounded in love, and a new reality for God's people is shaped in love. Steadfast love is the essence of discipleship.

In his meditations on the Gospel of John, William Temple insists that this is a call to the whole Church, indeed that this text shapes the mission of the Church![2] Amid the mystery and challenge of the Johannine Epilogue, the disciples find new direction for their lives. Amid the wonder of God's appearing, calls to ministry are cherished, obediently held, steadfastly embraced, and lived in the imaginations of these our biblical ancestors.

And what of our imaginations, are they strong enough to hear that pressing, poignant question: *Do you love me?* Will we respond with steadfast love, with denial, or with passivity? Are we bold enough to be

---

2. William Temple, *Readings in St. John's Gospel* [first published in 1939–40] (Wilton, Conn.: Morehouse Barlow, 1985), 377–388.

"obedient," that is to "hear," to "listen" to the calls to service that follow baptism? Sure, it was long ago when most of us emerged from the waters of baptism. Have we grown too old, too busy, too unimaginative to be renewed through this discipleship of love?

Do you love me? This is a tough question to live with, particularly in our own days. Our contemporary culture is not respectful of love. As a society we are often embarrassed by "love." Even saying the word, let alone thinking deeply about what it might mean for us, can make us stumble and turn away. Many confuse love with sentimentality, with fleeting romance, with an emotion that passes by now and then. The popular media have become extraordinarily adept at portraying *violence*. This is our strong cultural suit! Feminist author bell hooks reminds us that "We all know what violence looks like."[3] Yet we remain clumsy about imagining the profundity, the steadfast character of love. We all have tough, demanding work ahead if the Church we proclaim is actually to be filled with truth and love.

So here's a second story drawn from the treasury of historical witness, a story designed to refresh and renew our baptismal imaginations, a story about a woman who found not sentimentality but an abiding answer in love. Julian of Norwich, a fourteenth-century English woman, is beloved by Christians throughout the world. The clarity of her witness is found in a series of visions that later generations entitled *Revelations of Divine Love*.[4] This young, single recluse lived with steadfast dedication to her visions as a gift of God, a gift to be shared. Medieval women and men were much less shy about naming the holy in their midst, about claiming their own post-resurrection appearances. They loved the smallest details of God's appearing, the full gamut of emotions, the close encounters, the colorful sights, the ringing sounds and abundant odors of sanctity, the longed-for touch and the desired embrace. Julian tells us that she knew, we might say "experienced," God's abiding presence in her body, mind, and spirit.

She speaks without blushing of a divine love that tenderly "clothes, enfolds and embraces us." Apparently her contemporaries were not surprised (unlike some who today insist upon narrow modern orthodoxies) when she spoke of God as Father and God as Mother, and of the motherhood of God revealed in "Mother Jesus." The wonderfully evocative

---

3. bell hooks, *All About Love: New Visions* (New York: William Morrow and Company, 2000), 95.

4. I have used the modern English translation by Clifton Wolters of Julian's *Revelations of Divine Love* (Harmondsworth, Middlesex, England: Penguin Books, 1966); sections quoted are from chapters 5, 58-64, and 86.

language centers on the truth that, above all, God is love. Listen to a series of questions and responses—not unlike today's Gospel epilogue—that explain steadfast love as the meaning of God's revelations:

Who showed it thee? Love. What showed he thee? Love. Wherefore showed it he? For love. These responses are palpably saturated in love. In Julian's presence, to know God is to be surrounded by incredible love. This love is so profound and reassuringly confident that one line from Julian still echoes today: "All shall be well, and all shall be well, and all manner of thing shall be well!" Like the Johannine epilogue, Julian's revelation is clearly written, marked by great reverence, full of teaching about the Church's mission, and saturated in love. This simple medieval woman was extraordinarily adept at imagining the steadfast character of divine love.

And what about contemporary theologians? Who among us are Julian's equals as portrayers of divine love? Where are the prophets of just love today? Younger members of this assembly might rightly point to the non-violent and loving prophecies of the Zen master, Thich Nhat Hanh. Yet for me, as a child of the 1960s, there is one voice that still rings with poignant testimony, great reverence, and prophetic teaching about the Church's mission. In 1963, Dr. Martin Luther King Jr. published a now classic collection of his sermons entitled *Strength to Love*. This collection, including sermons written while Dr. King was in Georgia jails, bears reading and rereading for its passionate call to embrace forgiveness and love in community. By love, Dr. King was *not* speaking "about some sentimental or weak response." Rather he was speaking about love as a "moral imperative," as the "supreme unifying principle of life," about "love in action," and love *as* action. Cynics and sentimentalists take note: "Jesus is not an impractical idealist: he is *the* practical realist,"[5] Dr. King insisted. He spent his days, his life, proclaiming what love looks like!

What then is the meaning of these biblical, historical and contemporary visions for the new commitments to baptism and episcopacy set before us on this day? Love is what we hear as we emerge from the waters of birth and of baptism. My parish priest repeatedly reminds us that God is a "profligate lover" and a lavish giver of the Church's mission.[6] In baptism all people are named and receive a call to ministry. All are given gifts needed to fulfill the service set before them. "Nothing can surpass the gifts bestowed on [us] in birth and interpreted through

---

5. Dr. Martin Luther King Jr., *Strength to Love* [first published in 1963] (Philadelphia: Fortress Press, 1981), p. 50. See also Bell Hooks, *All About Love*, 74–77.

6. The Rev. Robert B. Appleyard, Jr. of Saint Barnabas Episcopal Church, Falmouth, Massachusetts.

baptism."[7] All are honored. All are loved! There are practical, realistic, and demanding challenges ahead for us *all* if we are to shape a Church that is truly steadfast in love. Thus the preacher's traditional "charge" to the ordinand will be followed today with a few concluding desires for us all.

Bud, I have three challenges for you:

1) As we deepen our vision that baptism is the source of all ministry, I encourage you to help this Church redefine *where* we look for authority. Help us pay apostolic attention to those we have not heard (or cared to hear) from before: to children, youth, and young adults; to neglected populations, races, and creeds; and to incarnate religious realities fraught with ambiguity, paradox, and even nonconformity. This will seldom be popular work, yet it could lead to an even more extraordinary Church!

2) I know you to be a skilled Christian educator, one truly knowledgeable about the manners and mysteries of this Church. Yet as a historical theologian, I challenge you, as you settle into that episcopal chair, to sit loose to tradition when it contradicts God's steadfast and compassionate love for God's people. New occasions do teach new duties. Help us keep abreast of truth as we glimpse the Holy in our midst.

3) The unity promised in baptism and "guarded" by bishops challenges us to overcome all that alienates and divides humanity. Lead us as a Church into an ethic of love in action . . . where power is shared, not hoarded among elites. Only then will we realistically and practically embody the fullness of God's steadfast love.

Sisters and brothers in Christ, I have three concluding aspirations for us all. I invite us:

1) To renew our commitment to a Church where all members, not just a few designated leaders, struggle in love to understand and live out the faith. Follow Jesus, the forgiving, compassionate lover, *the* practical realist. Wade more deeply into the baptismal waters of ministry.

2) To join in building a new Church that actually *is* grounded in baptism and not in ordination. This may be a novel experience for many of us, clergy and laity alike! We will all need to be diligent in learning that gifts and orders of ministry are beloved of God not because they are in the possession of any one person, but because they are shared in the body of Christ.

3) To become much more adept at making our sanctuaries places that foster imagining and living the steadfast character of divine love. In our

---

7. L. William Countryman, *Living on the Border of the Holy: Renewing the Priesthood of All* (Harrisburg, Pa.: Morehouse, 1999), 193.

society, which seemingly worships violence, we must demand images that reflect love's profound reality.[8]

Together let us embrace, teach, and practice a Christic, counter-cultural mission of steadfast love.

What an exciting time, what an extraordinary mission! What an appropriate moment to become more compassionate members of the Body of Christ! May God bless us all.

Fredrica Harris Thompsett is Mary Wolfe Professor of Historical Theology in the Episcopal Divinity School, Cambridge, Massachusetts.

This sermon was preached at the ordination of Roy F. (Bud) Cedarholm Jr. as Bishop Suffragan for the Diocese of Massachusetts.

---

8. bell hooks, *All About Love*, 95.

RENEWAL OF ORDINATION VOWS

Owning Our Vocation

Mark 11:15-19
Frederick W. Schmidt

THERE IS LITTLE wonder that this part of Mark's Gospel is not among the lections for ordination! Tables, chairs, moneychangers, and the odd pigeon flying. "You have made my house a den of robbers." The story hardly lends itself to occasions of celebration.

The mind races to think of what some might make of it, if invited to use it in the ministry of the Word at an ordination. I remember a conversation with a Methodist layman on the Oxfordshire Circuit who, I am convinced, would put it to *good* use. I discovered that the Circuit relied on three clergy to serve twenty-one churches. I asked how one could possibly provide pastoral care in a setting of that kind. "Oh, that's not a problem," he responded. "Clergy are like fertilizer. Spread them around and things grow. Put too much of it in one place and it just kills things."

But Holy Week brings us here, and we are beyond being hailed as bright young things embracing God's call. So perhaps there's a gift to be had in renewing our vows at this time of the year and in focusing on this Gospel reading. To do that, though, we need to look beyond three uses that people have made of this passage.

It is not, as some have thought, an indictment of Judaism, the Temple, or Temple worship. Fear, hatred, and prejudice have shaped this use of the text, which overlooks the obvious. Jesus was a Jew, speaking to Jews. His own practice brought him and his disciples to the Temple.

Nor is the focus of Mark's story christological. Jesus is not occupying the Temple, or declaring himself as its successor. An action of that kind would have precipitated a final confrontation between Jesus and Israel's overlords in an instant. In any event, Jesus addresses himself to proper use of the Temple, not to its elimination.

Nor is the story an indictment of money-grubbing in the Temple. As popular as this reading continues to be, there is more than one argument against it. One arises out of the circumstances surrounding worship in the first century. If you are going to offer an unblemished sacrifice at the Temple and you are traveling from any distance, you can hardly lug it over your shoulders all the way to Jerusalem. There needs to be some mechanism for getting a sacrifice to give. In holy precincts you can hardly use the profane coin of the realm. So, there needs to be a place where you buy animals and a mechanism for changing money. Taken on its own terms, objecting to animals and money changing at the Temple is a bit like objecting to asphalt around modern churches. Given the circumstances, you can hardly avoid it.

English translations and cultural lenses also contribute to misreading. The phrase "den of robbers" conjures up images of money-grubbing. But near contemporary use in Mark's day of the phrase "den of robbers" indicates that translators should use the words, "den of violent ones," "den of brigands," or even "members of the national liberation front."[1]

What then *is* the nature of the debate implied in the actions taken by Jesus? The issue, as nearly as we can tell, had to do with defining the nature of Israel's vocation and the symbolic place of the Temple in that vocation. For those who controlled the Temple's precincts, holiness and the separateness of Israel captured the essence of the nation's task. Changing profane coinage for sacred coinage in order to buy the appropriate sacrifices for use in the Temple helped preserve those boundaries. In the volatile political atmosphere of first-century Israel, these practices extended the resistance to Rome in powerfully symbolic terms.

By contrast—and in protest—Jesus insists that the Temple is a "house of prayer for all the nations." In a world wherein there were, from the Jewish point of view, only two kinds of people—Jews and the rest of the world—the meaning could not have been clearer. If for some of his contemporaries the future of the nation could be summarized in terms of a holy separation,

---

1. Marcus Borg, *Conflict, Holiness & Politics in the Teachings of Jesus* (New York: The Edwin Mellen Press, 1984), 174–5.

for Jesus the message of the Kingdom is a merciful contagion. The gospel is a word of hope to all, opening not just the Court of the Gentiles, but the entire Temple precinct to those inside and outside of Israel. Both his actions and words are part of a prophetic act designed to underscore that message. The chief priests and scribes had, from Jesus' point of view, redefined their vocation and that of the nation in ways that were alien and unacceptable.

In arriving there, they undoubtedly had the best possible motives. There is little doubt that the chief priests and scribes viewed the holiness of God and their definition of Temple worship as a sacred trust. To safeguard the Temple was to safeguard the worship of God. To safeguard the worship of God was to safeguard something sacred and essential about themselves. The chief priests and scribes did both.

If we put ourselves in their position—as we might on a day like this—their motives are completely intelligible and the dynamic entirely familiar. To be called is to hear the voice of God, and to hear the voice of God is to give definition and shape to one's life and work. As necessary as that task is, however, the reverse doesn't necessarily follow. The specifics of God's call in *one* moment do not shape or exhaust the will of God in *every* moment to come. In fact, God has an annoying habit of refusing to be captured in this way.

That there is spiritual peril in making the assumption that God can be so captured is not difficult to document. Some time ago I was asked to teach a course in an adult class at a Lutheran church. Since I find satisfaction in teaching, I agreed immediately. But almost as quickly I regretted saying yes. The class had a book they wanted me to use: *Scandals of the Faith*. A bit of Church-history muckraking, it was devoted to recounting less than admirable moments in Church history. Among others, it included chapters on the Inquisition, the Crusades, Luther's anti-Semitic leanings, and the conduct of Lutheran churches in the South prior to the Civil War. Given the efforts we were making to be nice to Lutherans, I was keen to avoid contributing to the failure of Anglican-Lutheran dialogue. But stories of this kind from Church history—theirs and ours—illustrate our tendency to enshrine in behavior certain understandings of God's will, and the evil that results. To be sure, some things done by our forebears in the name of Christ will be described as "understandable, given the times." But even at this distance from such events, it is impossible not to admit that genuine harm and evil were also done.

Profoundly sobering is the realization that our own definitions of vocation, and the impact they have on the life of the Church, will one day fall under similar scrutiny. Will the Church of another generation judge that we faithfully represented the will of God in our own day? Will our lives be marked by the freedom that Jesus displayed in hearing anew the voice of God? Or will our definitions of vocation be narrowly captured by an ideology that refuses to hear God in the way ideology captured the scribes and chief priests?

The answer, I think, will lie in part with the way we define the nature of ordained ministry in the early decades of the new millennium. The last four decades of the twentieth century were shaped by discoveries that deepened our understanding of the gospel and its movement in the lives of people. But each insight also tended to dominate how we defined ministry. And each definition brought along its own ideology.

In the sixties the prophetic mode dominated. We alerted the Church to profound social inequities and rightly so. But we often lost sight of the theological moorings of that undertaking, and the shape of our message took on a largely political cast. In the seventies and eighties we discovered that people were often defeated by emotional needs that went unaddressed. Here again, there was much to learn. But we gave ourselves so completely to unlicensed therapeutic practice that the larger spiritual and sacramental aspects of healing were all but lost. In the nineties, driven in part by the all-pervading influence of business, and spurred on by declining numbers, we gave ourselves to the entrepreneurial model of ministry. Here we still live today. To argue that we had much to learn about leadership is to belabor the obvious. But simply to style ourselves as the chief operating officers at branches of a multi-national organization is seriously deficient.

Missing from all three movements (and likely to be missing from any other movement) is the language of divine encounter and a sense of God's immediacy that seem to have been at the heart of Jesus' own experience. Ask what Jesus thought of the law, or the Temple, and you can define the position he took in sharply contradictory terms. But the problem, it seems to me, is not with inconsistency on Jesus' part, or with the nature of the literature, it lies instead with the nature of our questions.

We want to know what position Jesus took and ask, "What would Jesus do?" We quickly cast the moment in terms that can capture the shape of the future. But Jesus was interested in what God intended. Were we to see our responsibility in those terms, our approach to vocation would be very different. To nurture a space wherein divine encounter can take place requires humility and openness. It requires devotion to the deepening of an experience we cannot control or program. It requires a willingness to risk ourselves and the momentary *definitions* of God's will we craft in the interest of *knowing* God's will more fully. It involves knowing peril in much the same way that Jesus must have experienced his own prophetic act in the Temple as perilous.

This is not an easy invitation to hear. Ordained life is difficult enough that inviting added struggle seems masochistic. A long-time friend and devoted layman once told me, "Fred, the life of Episcopal clergy was, at one time, a life of genteel poverty. It is now no longer genteel." But to balk at the invitation is to focus on the professional and to neglect the vocational. Jesus clearly believed that the Temple could be a different place and that, by extension, the chief priests and scribes could play a different role. What convincing reason can we finally give for neglecting the invitation?

A pilgrim was walking down a road one day when he passed what seemed to be a monk sitting in a field. Nearby, men were working on a stone building. "You look like a monk," the pilgrim said. "I am that," said the monk. "Who is that working on the abbey?" "My monks," said the man. "I am the abbot." "Oh, that's wonderful," the pilgrim said. "It's so good to see a monastery going up." "We're tearing it down," the abbot said. "Tearing it down?" the pilgrim cried. "Whatever for?" "So we can see the sun rise at dawn," the abbot said.[2] May God grant us the courage and vision to imagine such a response.

Frederick W. Schmidt is Director of Spiritual Life
and Formation in the Perkins School of Theology,
Southern Methodist University, Dallas, Texas.

---

2. Joan Chittister, *The Fire in These Ashes: A Spirituality of Contemporary Religious Life* (Franklin: Sheed and Ward, 1995), 77.

5

MOTHERS' DAY

People Is People

John 13:34-36
Elizabeth M. Kaeton

FROM EPISCOPAL PULPITS in churches around the country this morning priests are either completely ignoring this day or piously lecturing how the Church does not celebrate secular holidays like Mother's Day or Father's Day. Yet we have hymns and prayers for national holidays in our prayer book and hymnal. And we remember the lives of saints whose lives were very secular. Such summary dismissals, therefore, cannot be the whole truth.

Truth be told, for some of us, Mother's Day, like Father's Day, is filled with more than a measure of discomfort. For some of us it is the pain of having lost our mothers to death. For others, it's the pain of having our mothers still alive but with a relationship, if not painful, less than satisfactory. Some of us are sitting here, filled with dread about this afternoon's visit or tonight's dinner. For many of us, it's about being a mother with a less-than-satisfactory relationship with our own children. Many of us live with the regret of never having had children, or of having lost a child, or the lingering pain and shame of a child long ago given up for adoption—or sacrificed to abortion. Others of us may have never been biological mothers but have deep, satisfying relationships with children who might just as well be our own. Others may know women—or men—who are more like mothers than our own biological mothers could ever be.

None of us is exempt from the messy complications of family relationships. It becomes clear, suddenly, why it is much easier to put the matters of Church before matters of family. There is a comforting kind of salve that comes from imposing the rules of the Church on the breaks and pains of one's heart! Into all of the complications of modern life, the ancient words of Jesus come rushing like a cool wind on a hot day: "A new commandment I give to you, that you love one another; even as I have loved you, that you also love one another. By this all will know that you are my disciples, if you have love for one another."

Mind you, Jesus says all these things immediately after Judas betrays him with a kiss. He tells them these things, then bids them farewell before he is brought to trial, condemned, and crucified. What a remarkable man! No wonder he was the Son of God. No human could ever live up to those standards. Could they?

Let me tell you about a man who became father and mother in God to me. His name was Father Koumaranian. He was an Armenian Orthodox priest. I was newly ordained and absolutely full of beans in my new position as Chaplain at the University of Lowell in Massachusetts. The Armenian Orthodox Church does not ordain women, but Father Koumaranian was, apparently, enchanted with me. He had decided that, since I seemed to have some pastoral skills and knew a little Hebrew and Greek, as well as having a fair comprehension of the Scriptures, that I might actually be redeemable as a priest. He was determined that if I was going to preside at divine liturgy, by God, I was going to learn the right way—the *orthodox* way.

It started slowly. He would call me up on a Wednesday and say, "Mother, this is Father. We are having wedding on Saturday. It would be good for you to learn liturgy. It would be good for my people to see woman priest. You come." It was more a command than an invitation. I went. Of course, I went. It was wonderful—the incense, the chanting, the strange incantations. I loved it!

One day, he called me up and said, "Mother, this is Father. We are having funeral tomorrow. It would be good for you to learn liturgy. It would be good for my people to see woman priest. You come."

The funeral service was filled with the same mystery and grandeur that marked every liturgy—Sunday Eucharist, weddings, or baptisms. The only thing changed was the makeup of the congregation. This one was filled with men in somber black coats and row upon row of women dressed from head to toe in black—complete with black scarves tied securely under their ample chins.

It came time for the eulogy. I assumed Father would speak to the congregation in Armenian, so I was a bit taken aback to hear him begin to speak in English. "There are people in this world," he said, "who are always making you happy. They are always having a smile, or a kind word to say. They are always doing a nice thing. Just to see them on the street makes your heart burst into song, so happy do they make you to see them." He walked over to the casket and put his hand lovingly on the top and said, "This . . . is not one of those people."

I was stunned! All I could think of was, "Please! Don't let anyone be able to read what my face is saying." My next thought was, "What the heck is he doing?" I opened my eyes and looked over at the first row of women where the man's wife sat. All the women, the entire row, were nodding their heads in agreement.

Then, I heard Father say, "But isn't our God so good, isn't our God so forgiving, that now, even now, this man is resting in eternal light in the loving arms of God, beloved of our Savior, Jesus Christ, and blessed by the warmth of the Holy Spirit. Because," he added, "people is people, and God is God."

In that one moment, Father Koumaranian taught me more about the love of God in Christ than any one of my fancy-schmancy courses in seminary: "People is people, and God is God." So, stop putting such high and divine expectations on each other, and love one another as God loves us.

It's so easy to miss the point that if there's a Christ in me and a Christ in you, then there's a bumbling, stumbling, saying-all-the-wrong-things Peter in me and a Peter in you. And there's a doubting Thomas in me and a doubting Thomas in you. And there's a scrupulous tax-collecting-putting-details-before-people Matthew in me, and a Matthew in you. And there's a betraying Judas in both of us.

People is people, and God is God. We all make messes in our lives, of our lives, and in other people's lives. We don't mean to, but there it is. We hurt the very people we love, and betray our best intentions to do otherwise. The more we detest our own imperfections, the more we seem to demand perfection from others. What we fear most in ourselves, we hate most in others. Into these dilemmas, Father Koumaranian says, "People is people, and God is God."

So, if you are worried about your Mother's Day celebration—for whatever reason—or about the fact that the Church's denial of reality won't make it any better. Relax. God doesn't expect the same perfection you—or this culture—expect of you or others. Because God was in Christ, God knows our humanness, even better than we do. God knows our limitations as well as our possibilities. And God still loves us very, very much.

Just remember this: Into these modern times come the ancient words of Jesus, "A new commandment I give to you, that you love one another; even as I have loved you, that you also love one another. By this all will know that you are my disciples, if you have love for one another."

Elizabeth M. Kaeton is Rector of St. Paul's Church,
Chatham, New Jersey.

MEMORIAL DAY
THE SUNDAY AFTER ASCENSION DAY

Remembering Our Dead

John 17
Arthur L. Sargent

IN THE CHURCH'S calendar of feasts and fasts, last Thursday was the Feast of the Ascension, which celebrates the Good News that after his death and resurrection, Jesus ascended into the heavens to sit at the right hand of the Father. For most of us, this may sound poetic but far removed from the way we understand ourselves. Such was not the case with people of the first century. People in the first-century Mediterranean world knew themselves to be surrounded by a host of spiritual beings of various ranks and powers. Gods, demigods, angels, semidivine heroes and lesser spiritual beings—powers, authorities, and dominions—inhabited the land just as surely as humans did. In the scheme of things, humans were little more than the playthings of these beings who pursued jealous squabbles involving intrigues for power, sexual seduction, and revenge of such ornate intricacy as to make the plots of soap operas look not only unimaginative but decorous in comparison.

As bizarre as we may find these stories to be, people of the first century did not find them amusing, for they knew themselves to be mere pawns in the divine intrigues. They also knew that the gods were at best indifferent, at worst hostile, to humans—and always unpredictable. That world was the context in which the early Church proclaimed that, forty days after his Resurrection, Jesus ascended into the heavens to be seated at the right hand of the Father. The message of the Ascension is that the powers, authorities, and dominions of this Age, whether they masquerade as temptations to personal sin or as ideologies of economic, political, or social structures, the powers who controlled human existence have been vanquished by a far more powerful divine energy given to us in Christ Jesus. Good News indeed!

The vanquishing of the powers of this age is as good of a theme as any to serve as an introduction to the topic of Memorial Day, a time this nation has set aside to remember its war dead. For many folks honoring our war dead seems inconsistent with a gospel of love and peace. No doubt some of this unease is linked to a laudable desire to respect the ancient Christian teachings against war. No doubt this unease, in some cases, is exacerbated by the depth and intensity of the political and social divisions of the Vietnam era, the scars of which remain with us to this day. The honesty and love we owe one another dictate that we honor this unease, even as we recognize that the context of the Church's ancient pacifist teachings was quite different from our own.

Ancient Christians lived in a social and political context in which people (with the exception of a small number of noble families) were the personal possessions of an emperor who could do with them as he saw fit. War and soldiering were what emperors did, and they did them ruthlessly. In such a context an ethic that rejected war and service in a military that was typified by rape, torture, murder, and plunder was practically a self-evident moral imperative.

We, however, live in a representative democracy, and regardless of how much we might like to divorce ourselves of all responsibility for actions of the state, as long as we remain citizens, we remain responsible for taking the sometimes morally dubious actions necessary to maintain the social order. Furthermore, because of the wealth and power of our country, we, as a nation, are largely responsible for the well-being and order of the world. It may make moral sense for a small, powerless minority in an empire ruled by a ruthless aristocratic oligarchy to reject the use of force, but in our time and place such abdication of responsibility is morally defensible only by the rare individual called to make an individual witness against the inherent injustices of this age.

Those few are to be honored and treasured. The rest of us, for better or worse, like it or not, have the moral responsibility to not only confront the blood-stained face of history but to engage the moral ambiguity of that history in an effort to make it a little less bloody. Too frequently, that engagement will mean war in all its horror and moral uncertainty. Whenever the Republic makes war, the majority will inevitably send fellow citizens to war, and some of those we send will die. Thus it is we are obligated to remember those who have died in the wars we have waged, whether or not we approve of war in principle or of a specific war such as Vietnam.

Remembering our war dead is a bittersweet business. It is bitter in its focus on the individual, who more often than not was cut off from the land of family and loved ones as a young person—quite probably little more than a child. It is bitter to see in the mind's eye young beautiful bodies made for joy and the love of life mangled and destroyed in the moral fog and gore of combat. It is bitter in that every war, even the most noble fought for the most righteous reasons, involves the most horrendously cruel and merciless actions and degradation of all that is good and admirable in our race. It is bitter in that the few suffer and die for the many.

Remembering is sweet in that, if we are willing to receive it, the dead have a gift to give us. From the earliest of times, humans have intuitively known that when men and women are caught up in events beyond their control or making, and suffer and die in solidarity, they are elevated above common human existence into the realm of heroes. As heroes, they can be models for the living on how to endure, and this is the gift they offer us. This fundamental truth of human existence is at the root of all stories we tell over and over again about the heroes of both history and mythology.

We, the living, are obligated to remember, and in our remembering we are duty bound to pray for the dead. Since some of us are from religious traditions that do not offer prayers for the dead, let me explain why this church prays for the dead. We do so because we hold the dead in our love, and we trust that in God's loving care, they will grow in his love and in communion with us. Our prayers are an expression of our continuing love and communion. We, the living, are also obligated to protect the memory of the dead from being exploited by the powers and authorities of this age for their own selfish purposes. The war dead are to be remembered for themselves alone. They are their own reason and justification for both our remembering and our prayers.

Those who remember the war dead as a means of glorifying the state or any ideology or any institution or any worldly power cheapen and dishonor the heroic status the dead have received by their suffering and death, and in so doing they are revealed as tools of those very powers, authorities, and dominions that have been vanquished by the ascended Christ Jesus.

Meanwhile, we remember, and we pray. In so doing, we strengthen the ongoing fellowship we have with them and with one another. In the continuing fellowship we also strengthen the bonds of love that bind us together in a unity—a unity Jesus prayed for on the night of his betrayal, a unity that transcends whatever individual differences of opinion we may have about the morality of war.

Remembering, we pray: Rest eternal grant to them, O Lord. And let light perpetual shine upon them.

Arthur L. Sargent is Priest Associate at St. James' Church,
Taos, New Mexico.

FOURTH OF JULY

God's Freedom Bell

Deuteronomy 10:17-21; Hebrews 11:8-16
Douglas Hahn

THIS IS A DAY of gathering, remembering, and feasting. A day for declaring freedom and ringing bells. We are celebrating Independence Day. You will hear much today about our freedom from tyranny, the birth of our independence, and our calling to be a new nation. These things are good to remember. There is another part of this celebration—something we as a Church can and should proclaim as loudly as anything else we hear this day. While we are all declaring our independence, I invite us also to declare our *dependence*—our dependence on God and on one another.

A declaration of *dependence* would be true to the events of July 4, 1776. When the thirteen little fledgling colonies declared *independence* from Great Britain that day, they were also declaring their *dependence* on one another. Not one of them could stand by itself against that great power. They all needed the help and support of the others. The founding leaders in Philadelphia spent much energy holding together their fragile alliance. They knew they could succeed in this venture only if they cast their hopes for the future upon their common cause. They had to be united. Their hopes and their lives depended on it. How did Benjamin Franklin express it? *We must hang together or we will surely hang separately!*

That is important for us to remember and declare today. We must hang together and, more importantly, together cling to God if we are to survive. A friend of mine refers to the year of his birth as "when I discovered America." He is making a serious point. We arrive as strangers to this strange place, little aliens with hearts full of hope and need, mostly open arms and mouths. We depend on a mother's arms to care for us, a father's hands to nurture us. Were we not welcomed, we would not survive. We need "life support" from the start. The Bible knows that this "life support" comes from God's own heart. We are welcomed and we live.

Our ancestors depended on God when they were in a new land. "You were once strangers in Egypt" says the writer of Deuteronomy. They knew they were "only strangers and nomads on earth," says Hebrews. These words are echoed through our Scripture. Our spiritual ancestors confessed that they had been wanderers and strangers who had survived only because of God's good welcome.

And like our "alien" Hebrew ancestors, we survive each day because of God's good welcome. The air we breathe, the water that flows freely to our homes—these are continuing signs of God's hospitality. It is as if each morning God says to us, "Welcome, my special guest! Have some food; have some clothes. My home is your home!"

And as part of that welcome, God's mercy has placed us in human community. An infant left alone will not survive; neither will we live long without human support. We depend on one another—friends and kind strangers with whom God has placed us. Think of your dependence on others in something as common as your morning breakfast. The coffee beans, fruit, and bread were grown by a farmer somewhere far away. A truck driver drove long hours to deliver them to sale. A clerk woke extra early to deliver her baby to the daycare and get to the store so the doors could be open. Many hands delivered your first meal of the day and every meal you eat.

The Bible reminds us that these are flesh and blood extensions of God's own arms and hands. God's own good hands feed us and clothe us by the labors of others. And if the physical gifts from God's hands keep us alive, the spiritual gifts from God's hands make our living rich and meaningful. God's hands pull us together in love—making our communities, our families and church and neighborhood and nation. God's hands pull us apart when we are at each other's throats; they put us back together when we fall into sin and death. God's hands give us all we need. They have never been withdrawn. And even when, for some insanity, we bound these hands with nails, they came to us again, raising us to new life and new community.

This new life and new community is full of blessing and freedom. In this mutually dependent humanity we know true humanity. Isn't this the best gift of freedom—mutually dependent life? We often think of freedom in terms of what we are free *from*—tyranny, unjust taxes, and foreign governments. But the real promise of freedom lies in what we are free *for*. You and I are free for one another.

We are free to gather with one another for worship. Free to assemble for peace or protest. We are free to join our voices with others against that very state that preserves our freedom. Free to care for those who are without, or to welcome those who are strangers. We are free to join hands in a Habitat project with neighbors. God has given us freedom—for one another and for God's people around the world.

And the most radical freedom we have been given: freedom to love our enemy, that strangest of strangers. Is that freedom? Some may say we are just as free to hate our enemy. But that is not freedom. Martin Luther King reminded us that the first slave of hate is the one who hates. Have you ever been so obsessed with thoughts of revenge against someone that you were not free to think of anything else? Have you lain awake at night forming your next argument against an "enemy," or fantasizing about his or her demise? This may have seemed to satisfy some hunger, but I bet it didn't feel like freedom.

How blessed to be set free from the fear, suspicion, and score keeping of hating an enemy! What freedom to let this hatred go! To transform this energy into the energy of love. How freeing to respond as Abraham Lincoln did when asked how he planned to destroy the enemy after the war: "The best way to destroy an enemy is to make him my friend." We are set free from hate, set free for love.

When I was a child my grandmother had in her back yard in a large bell on a tall post connected to a long rope. Every neighbor seemed to have one just like it. At the beginning of my annual summer visits, Granny instructed me: "At dinner time, as I finish cooking, you go ring that bell three or four times. That will signal everyone to drop their work and come eat. One more thing," she would continue. "This is important. If something goes wrong—if I get hurt or if there is a fire—you ring that bell like your life depended on it. The neighbors know what that means, and they will come running to help."

I think of that bell every time I hear bells ring on the Fourth of July. I invite you to hear it too. This is the bell that bids all you who labor to drop everything and come. Let go of all with which you are heavy laden, including your hate for your enemies. This bell calls you to declare your dependence on God. It calls you to gather around these tables prepared for one another, and around Christ's own table where all you need is a hungry heart and open hands. It calls you to declare your dependence on one another. This bell that calls you to come to the aid of those who are hurt or whose lives are burning up. It calls you to let others declare their dependence on you.

This is the bell of God's freedom. It echoes God's mercy. It rings welcome to God's enemies and to ours. It sounds God's nurture and care. It rings for us and for the whole world. Let it ring! Let it ring! Let it ring!

Douglas Hahn is Rector of St. Thomas' Church, Columbus, Georgia.

THANKSGIVING DAY

Remembering in Abundance

Deuteronomy 8:1-3, 6-10
Melissa Q. Wilcox

I IMAGINE many of you wore Moses' sandals when you sent your kids off to college. Do you remember that day? On the long ride to school, you gave your child the final speech: Remember all those things we have taught you. Remember the family rules. Remember not to get mixed up in sex and drugs. And for God's sake, remember to call home. We know you will just love college—the freedom to stay up as late as you want, to order Domino's pizza at three in the morning, to go to classes dressed in your pajamas. But, don't forget who you are and where you have come from. After the speech, you spent hours hauling computer boxes, bean-bag chairs, clothes, and more clothes into your child's room. You said good-bye, kept a stiff upper lip, and then broke out the box of Kleenex when you got in the car. Meanwhile, your child waved to you from new life in the Promised Land. Letting go is hard, unnerving. Letting go involves vulnerability.

God must have felt vulnerable when he had Moses bring the Israelites to the Promised Land. After all, God had cut a covenant with the children of Israel—adopted them as his own. God led them out of Pharaoh's ugly grasp. In the wilderness, the relationship was tested and strengthened. After all, the Israelites went without the gourmet food of Egypt and got stuck with the generic manna that God rained down from heaven. What curious food—always enough for everyone, but no one could stockpile it for a rainy day! Of course, rain was another problem. Once the Israelites were so fed up with being thirsty that they had Moses strike a rock so that they could drink. In and through all of this, the relationship with God was so tight, so real. Each day the Israelites knew they had to wake up and put their whole trust in the Lord God. God had a captive audience. God did not have to work hard to be noticed or loved. Now God was going to let these people go into a lovely place where God might end up as an afterthought.

I think most of us have a sense of God's near presence in times of hardship, and God's not-so-near presence when things are going pretty well. When I lived in Tanzania, I often said extra prayers to God throughout the day. *Thank you, God, that the stomach bug I had yesterday turned out not to be amoebic dysentery. Thank you that we had enough rainwater collected to pour on the new garden. Thank you, God, for keeping that crazy bus driver from going too fast as that chicken scratched its foot on my head. God, please help Absalom while he lives without a salary. Please be with Neema while her mom has malaria. God, keep the mice out of my bed tonight.* The prayers and petitions went on from sunrise to sunset in a foreign land. When I came home, I noticed that my prayers changed. I still said my morning and evening prayers, but the little ones throughout the day got put aside. God had not changed. God had not gone on vacation. God was still waiting to be in conversation with me.

So, can you see why God might have some fears about actually letting the Israelites into the Promised Land? They might get to the point where the flowing streams would make it easy to forget who provided them with water in the desert, or those pomegranates and olive trees. That abundance of bread and honey might make it easy to forget who had fed them day in and day out for forty years with bread from heaven. The richness of the Promised Land is the confirmation of the covenant God cut with the Israelites. Now God fears that the very fulfillment of that covenant might lead Israel far from him.

Kathleen Norris writes about our inability to come to terms with how far we stray from God. Sometimes, we put God in the background even by the way that we confess our sins. She says, "I am a sinner, and the Presbyterian Church offers me a weekly chance to come clean, and to pray, along with others, what is termed a prayer of confession. But pastors can be so reluctant to use the word 'sin' that in church we end up confessing nothing except our highly developed capacity for denial. One week, for example, the confession began, 'Our communication with Jesus tends to be too infrequent to experience the transformation in our lives You want us to have,' which seems less a prayer than a memo from one professional to another. At such times I picture God as a wily writing teacher who leans across the table and says, not at all gently, 'Could you possibly be troubled to say what you mean?' It would be refreshing to answer, simply, 'I have sinned.'"[1]

The God of Moses is a vulnerable God who fears we might be kept from saying, "I have sinned" because of our abundance. For many of us,

---

1. Kathleen Norris, *Amazing Grace* (New York: Riverhead Books, 1998), 165.

Thanksgiving Day is filled with abundance. We may have already put a plump turkey in the oven. We have set a glorious table complete with candles and silver. The potatoes are peeled and ready to go. The pies will be thrown in the oven to warm at the end of the day. Thanksgiving Day is a holiday celebrating abundance. We often gather to look back on the year to see our abundance. We see it in the faces of family and friends seated at the Thanksgiving table. We feel abundance at the end of the afternoon when our stomachs ache, and we long to stretch out for a nap. Abundance is a good thing—something for which we give thanks. How do we honor God in the midst of our abundance?

I think about the abundance that families of the Afghan Aid workers are feeling this year at Thanksgiving. The pastor at the American women's church, upon hearing of their release, said, "Thanksgiving has come early in Islamabad." Can you imagine the abundance they must feel? After being locked in a container ninety miles south of Kabul and hearing bombs around them, surely the workers feared for their lives. Then, to their surprise, early one morning the doors burst open. They thought the Taliban were going to kill them. Instead, the men were Northern Alliance soldiers shouting freedom. They flew out of that container and were met with joy, laughter, and hugs from Afghan people. God was in the midst of that abundance. Even more amazing was an unexpected source of light so that the U.S. could airlift them to Pakistan. The light from the available lanterns, necessary to guide the helicopters, was so bleak that the aid workers, six of whom were women, threw off their traditional burkas and set them on fire. Soon other women in the village were doing likewise. God certainly lives in abundance. But abundance often comes after pain. C. S. Lewis says, "God whispers to us in our pleasures, speaks to us in our conscience, but shouts in our pains; it is his megaphone to rouse a dead world."[2]

These aid workers certainly heard God's megaphone as they lived and waited. I suspect that they will also live closely with God in their abundance as well. How do we, people who may not have lived with such drama, live into God's abundance? We have chosen to gather to thank God with the Great Thanksgiving on this Thanksgiving Day. For in God's Son we have true abundance. We have reason to gather every week and celebrate abundance of life. In God's Son, we gather around a simple table clothed in abundance. Not one covered with turkey,

---

2. C. S. Lewis, *The Problem of Pain* (New York: Macmillan, 1944; New York: Harper Collins, 2001), 91.

potatoes, pies, and pop, but gathered around one loaf of bread and one cup of wine. In God's Son, we gather with the one who cut a covenant with us. That covenant life celebrates our abundance in Christ Jesus. That covenant life reminds us not to forget God, even when we are surrounded with abundance. That covenant life calls us to remember God and God's commandments even when both feet are firmly planted in the Promised Land.

Melissa Q. Wilcox is Curate at The Church of the Holy Comforter, Kenilworth, Illinois.

■ 6

COLUMBINE HIGH SCHOOL MASSACRE

Where Is God?

Jeremiah 23:1-6; Colossians 1:11-20
Doris Buchanan Johnson

THIS HAS BEEN a week of pain and horror. NATO has spent four weeks raining bombs on Kosovo. We look in disbelief at the photos pouring out of the country. Rivers of refugees walk away, carrying only the clothes on their backs. Streams of unsuspecting people are cut off as they rush to escape. Banks of dead men lie arrayed in ditches, shot at point-blank range. Fires light night skies. Homes and businesses are burned out. Seared craters remain where bombs have obliterated everything recognizable as life.

We are incredulous, horrified, overwhelmed. We can scarcely take it in. Humanity's inhumanity is a heinous scene!

Then, just when we think things can't get worse, they *do!* In a bastion of middle-class values and comfort, disaster strikes again! Two teens of the "trench-coat Mafia" stun us. They walk into their suburban high school and open fire on their classmates. Randomly choosing, they shoot some, spare others. "There's a jock. Waste him." "She believes in God? Bang, she's dead." "Black and popular? Get him good." The shooting rampage leaves fifteen dead, twice that number wounded.

Parents and families of the dead and injured wail, unbelieving. Hundreds of teens tremble with fear. Millions are horrified and outraged. We weep with the grieving parents. We want to rush to our own children, hold them, keep them safe. We shudder as this demonic terror invades our carefully constructed sanctuaries.

Wordlessly we plead that such terror never strike in our midst! We ask ourselves: When does it end?

Looking back over thousands of years, we can say with honesty—and alarm—it doesn't!

The impotence we now feel is not new. Truth is faithfully established, and continually undermined. Falsehoods stand unchallenged. Hatreds mount. Persecution unveiled leads, not to resolution, but to escalating cycles of uncontrollable violence. Where is God?!

Jeremiah struggles in such a world. Despite prophecies preceding him, the tyranny of the priesthood and kings continues. Wickedness and domination prevail. The world around Jeremiah is rife with treachery incited by corrupt leadership.

Just as in Kosovo, Judah's leadership has failed: circumstances go from bad to worse to unthinkable. Each inept leader is succeeded by another more incompetent, less insightful, more ruthless. Kosovo. Nazi Germany. Judah and Israel. Colorado. Nebuchadnezzar's army. Each is an icon of senseless killing and errant leadership. But it isn't simply the leadership. Society is ill. Individual craving wins out over community commitment. The poor and needy become expendable, victims of neglect. The scorned become desolate. The wealthy isolate themselves, unwilling to see. Those called to preach deliverance go unheeded.

God is calling, but no one hears. Jeremiah asks: When will it end? Where is God? Something utterly unique is called for—and given. The word of the Lord, spoken to Jeremiah, comes to afflicted people: "I will raise up a shepherd over them and they shall not fear any longer."

"The Lord God alone is our righteousness," Jeremiah declares. "Only *one* thing can save us from ourselves . . . the justice and love of God." Jeremiah promises that a Messiah, a branch of David, will spring up. This "anointed one" will arrive as surely as spring follows winter. The name of this Messiah will be "The Lord is our Righteousness," our justice, our judgment. The day is surely coming, Jeremiah tells us, a great day, one near at hand, when justice will reign. This is hope, proclaimed in the worst of times. But this hope comes from deep within: from faith in the past action of God and from faith in God's continuing promise.

The author of Colossians draws us further into the future: "The Father has rescued us from the power of darkness, and transferred us into the kingdom of his beloved Son." Our sustenance is encountered in the reality of our Messiah's presence. The Messiah is sent. God *is* with us. Both are in sight here and now. In Kosovo, in Colorado, God is here. . . grieving with us, holding us, leading us to the door of the empty tomb. Resurrection and redemption beckon, waiting for our response. God stands with us, and beyond us, in hope.

Certainly, our anguish and fear remain. We weep for lives cut short by ethnic cleansing and two unbalanced young men. We pray for victims and persecutors. We lament over the mistreated and the forgotten.

Unquestionably we can, and should, work in every way we know to teach respect, self-control, and inclusive vision. Nevertheless, our actions alone are insufficient. Not until we rest in the hope of the Lord will our hearts know the joy of true redemption and new creation.

We wonder how that looks. But we have only to observe. God is in Kosovo—in every person who stops to aid the exhausted to their feet, in the families in Macedonia and Albania who have opened their homes to total strangers, in the NATO troops who nightly place their lives on the line for the freedom of others.

God is in Littleton, Colorado—in the teacher who urges students to safety while taking no thought of his own, in the students who protect others before themselves, in the police who try to extricate students from the firestorm.

God's redemption and re-creation can be subtle or dramatic. Either way the Shepherd is among us—already.

Doris Buchanan Johnson is Associate Rector of St. John's Church,
Ellicott City, Maryland.

EXECUTION OF TIMOTHY McVEIGH

Finding Our Way Toward Forgiveness

Luke 7:36-50
Wanda Pizzonia

MONDAYS ARE my day off, precious time to unplug and to catch up on those proverbial things left undone. Last Monday morning, I awoke, hoping to spend the last Monday before the beginning of school vacation quietly and in peace. Easier said than done! A few minutes after 7 AM, I switched on *The Today Show,* where coverage of Timothy McVeigh's execution was in progress. Katie Couric sat solemnly before the nation. Behind her the sun shone brightly on a distant church steeple. Whether the choice of backdrop was coincidental or intentional, it seemed impossible to view the unfolding events without considering issues of faith.

Over the next half hour, a series of witnesses to the execution reported their observations of the morning's events. Viewers learned that just prior to his death, McVeigh looked one by one into the eyes of the witnesses, family members of the victims of the Oklahoma City bombing, and reporters. He then fixed his eyes on the ceiling and awaited the inevitable.

A nation wondered: In those last moments was he truly sorry for his actions? Did he want God's forgiveness and the forgiveness of his victims and their families? Some had hoped for a personal declaration of remorse, yet there was none. A handwritten copy of a defiant poem served as his final statement. Most reports suggested he remained cool and passionless to the end. Later, we would learn that, in a return to the faith of his childhood, McVeigh had invited a Catholic priest to administer last rites with anointing behind the closed curtain of the execution chamber just moments prior to his death. It is hard for any of us to imagine what might have been in the heart of Timothy McVeigh as he prepared to receive his sentence.

Still we wonder. Could God forgive even Timothy McVeigh? This morning, Luke's Gospel brings us face to face with Jesus' enormous capacity to forgive sin. Given the events of this past week and as we prepare to receive the Gospel through new eyes and ears, perhaps we would be wise to resist the human desire for a simple, definitive answer.

As we meet Jesus, he has come to eat dinner with Simon, the Pharisee, a man faithful to Jewish law and to the tenets of Hebrew Scripture. Simon and his guests recline at the table, leaning on their left elbows for support, their right hands free to eat the dinner before them. In the midst of the gathering, a woman enters the room uninvited, carrying an alabaster jar of ointment. The whispers begin. She is a sinner by reputation, although the specifics of her sins are not revealed. Whatever the nature of her past indiscretions, they are considered shocking. Her hair is loose. No proper woman comes into mixed company looking so suggestive. To make matters worse, she drops to her knees and pours ointment on Jesus' feet, a sign of honor. Oil and tears flow together. Without shame, she wipes both with her hair.

Simon, the proper host, wonders incredulously: "Doesn't he know what she's done? If this man were really God's prophet, he would know what kind of woman this is!" The clear inference is that *Simon* knows.

Following the custom of their time, Jesus poses a riddle: "Simon, two debtors owe money. One of them owes a significant sum; the other owes a small sum. Neither can pay, so both are forgiven what they owe. Who is more grateful?" The answer is obvious—the one with the larger debt. Jesus seems implicitly to suggest that the woman falls into this category. Is it possible that someone like Timothy McVeigh does also?

When we speak in abstract terms, it is easy to say that anyone can be forgiven. Yet, when we attach a face and a sentence to an individual it becomes more difficult to imagine that great sins can be forgiven. And so we ask, is there a limit to God's forgiveness?

Bud Welch, who has run a gas station in Oklahoma City for the past thirty-four years, has wrestled with that question since April 19, 1995. His daughter, Julie, was killed in the Oklahoma City bombing. He has shared details of

her life. She was born prematurely and struggled to survive, ultimately growing up healthy and strong. At the time of her death, she was a recent graduate of Marquette University, using her Spanish degree as a translator with the
Social Security Administration. She was dating an Air Force lieutenant named
Eric. Only after her death would her father learn that they had planned to
announce their engagement two weeks after the bombing occurred.

The pain Bud felt at losing Julie was overwhelming. He had been a life-
long opponent of the death penalty, a conviction that he had held even
as he imagined the worst that could happen. Even when friends suggested
that he might change his mind if something horrible happened to a loved
one, he couldn't imagine a change of heart. Then, the worst thing *did* happen. He found himself filled with "anger, pain, hatred and revenge."

Six months later, he was drinking and smoking heavily, and he knew he
had to take steps to regain control of his emotions. He visited the bombing
site. Initially, rage and anger swept over him, and he declared that anyone
responsible for such violence should be put to death. Over time, he began
to ask if McVeigh's execution would make any difference. The answer was
always the same: No. The death penalty would only return the hatred and
revenge that motivated the crime in the first place. Welch began traveling
around the country speaking against the death penalty.

Three years later, he went to visit Timothy McVeigh's family. He had
seen Bill McVeigh on television and recognized a father's pain in his eyes.
It took a lot of nerve to make the visit, and for the first thirty minutes of
their meeting, the two men talked and pulled weeds in the garden outside.
Then, the two walked together into the house to meet Jennifer McVeigh,
Tim's sister. There were family photographs on the wall in the kitchen. Bud
Welch couldn't take his eyes off the largest one. "Gosh," he said. "What
a good-looking kid." Bill McVeigh, who had only moments earlier confessed his difficulty at showing emotion, replied, "That's Tim's graduation
picture." A large tear rolled down his cheek. Later that day, as Bud Welch
prepared to leave, he shook Bill's hand and offered a hand to Jennifer.
Instead of returning his handshake, Jennifer reached out and hugged Bud's
neck. Both began to cry. Bud said, "Honey, we're in this together for the
rest of our lives. And we can make the most of it if we choose." Bud promised that he would do what he could to keep her brother alive. Later, he
reflected, "I've never felt closer to God than I did at that time. I felt like a
thousand pounds had been lifted from my shoulders."

Bud Welch did what seems incomprehensible, and yet he is quick to
share how difficult forgiveness has been. He notes, "Forgiveness is not
something you just wake up one morning and decide to do. You have to
work through your anger and your hatred as long as it's there. You have
to try to live each day a little better than before. I do have setbacks, even

when I'm sure that I want to forgive . . . How can it ever be over? A part of my heart is gone . . . "[1]

A recent cover article in *Newsweek* magazine made this observation:

"Scanning the family photographs of Timothy McVeigh, we see images of an apparently normal child, as ordinary as Sunday dinner with Grandma. Timothy McVeigh stands proudly behind his sister, plays with a model airplane, frolics in the swimming pool. But what America yearns to see is different; that the man the child has become is not a man at all, but a monster; doing so enables us to put him in a category labeled Evil with a capital E, but also, more importantly, one labeled 'not us.' We need to assure ourselves, to set him worlds apart from us."[2]

Simon the Pharisee certainly struggled to do this with the woman who unabashedly bathed and anointed Jesus' feet. He could see her sin, but had little self-awareness about his own need for forgiveness.

By God's grace, perhaps none of us will have to test our capacity for forgiveness on a large scale. But, how would we fare on a smaller scale if we were to bring a person who has wronged us around this table? Will an awareness of the love of God in us give us the freedom to forgive others?

We can imagine all sorts of things that can seem unforgivable: a childhood with an alcoholic parent, a betrayal, a marital conflict, a difficult work or family situation. We might resist any suggestion that the person who has wronged us deserves to be present at the table with Jesus. And yet, as surely as you and I have been offered a place at the Lord's Table, so also has the person who has done what seems unforgivable. Only by acknowledging God's deep love for us can we reach tentatively toward the forgiveness of others in our lives.

Kathleen Norris has written about the difficulty of forgiving sin in view of the presence of horrendous evil in the world.

"Like a child pulling up the covers to keep the monsters under the bed, we hide behind the mask of the self and say, 'I'm a good person.' One of the most challenging things about Jesus is the way that he pulls those covers back . . . If I am honest with myself . . . I am more realistic about seeing the mixture of good and evil in myself."[3]

The first step toward forgiveness of ourselves, and others, is to understand the power of God's love for us—not historic or distant, but rather

---

1. Bud Welch, "On Forgiving McVeigh," *Christian Science Monitor* (Vol. 93, Issue 138, June 11, 2001), 9ff.

2. Sharon Begley, Andrew Murr, Adam Rogers, "The Roots of Evil," *Newsweek* (Vol. 137, Issue 21, May 21, 2001), 30ff.

3. Kathleen Norris, *Amazing Grace: A Vocabulary of Faith* (New York: Riverhead Books, 1998), 176–7.

close, embracing, steadfast love. Love that can forgive anything that we have done, love that has the power to forgive what others have done to us. This morning as we wrestle with the real difficulty of forgiving others, may we first be overwhelmed with God's great love and forgiveness for us. Then, perhaps as that love and forgiveness overflow our hearts, we shall be free in ways yet unimagined to extend God's grace to those in our midst.

Wanda Pizzonia is Associate Rector of St. Luke's Church,
Darien, Connecticut.

MOURNING FOR VICTIMS OF SEPTEMBER ELEVENTH

What Are We Going to Do Now?

Isaiah 61:1-6; Psalm 27; Revelation 21:1-7; Matthew 5:1-16
David J. Schlafer

OH MY GOD! What are we going to do now? That is the question we instinctively ask when all of a sudden our world blows apart. *Oh my God! What are we going to do now?*

The *first* time we ask the question—as fireballs flare and towers collapse—the answer is spontaneous, thoughtless, wordless. Our bodies do the talking: hearts pound, faces freeze, muscles jerk. We do not pause to consider the options—the answer is automatic: *What are we going to do now? Duck and run! Get out of here!*

But there is more to this question than a first response can give. It comes again, a second time: *What are we going to do* now? And maybe because it's our job, what we get paid to do, but more likely because it springs from an instinct as deep as self-protection, a second answer comes to the second asking: *What are we going to do now? Reach out and help!*

Not much calculation in this response either. "It'll look great on my resume." "My mother will be so proud." "Tough job, but good pay." No, none of the above. Rather, the raw imperative of pure human freedom: "They're in danger; I gotta go. I must do something—whatever I can— whatever it takes!"

But the question doesn't go away with Answer Number Two. Indeed, the very answer offered in heroic rescue action *rekindles* the question with greater force: "Limited success, dwindling hope, lives lost, loves torn"— *What are we going to do now?*

And another answer makes its way into our asking space, still spontaneous, but now more measured: *Mourn and weep.* And so we have done, since unforgettable Tuesday, wells of tears brimming in our eyes, floods of tears falling from our eyes—eyes of all ages, all races, all religions (and no religion). Eyes of women, eyes of men (unashamed tears from males, for a change). Tears of grandfathers, aunts, children, neighbors; tears of citizens from many nations. Every tear appropriate—no tear wasted.

Has anyone ever told you: "That's nothing to cry over!" "There, there. Don't cry." Or "You stop that crying, right this minute!"? Well, maybe someone has at some time or another. But I'll bet they *haven't* said such things to you in the last few days. *Oh my God! What are we going to do now? Mourn and weep.*

Mourn and weep—but once again, the answer regenerates the question. So many people mourning and weeping—*What are we going to do now?* As the question goes deeper, a deeper answer comes as well. *Hug and hold.* Stricken though you are, you can embrace the stricken. You don't have to flash a "no scars" badge. Your own scars credential you for hugging and holding the wounded and weeping.

But after that, then what? *What are we going to do now?* A cascade of options spills across the mental screen. *Storm and rage! Strike back! Hunker down! Put it behind you and just get on!* So many options, none without reason, not all contradictory—but not all compatible. And *this* may be why we have witnessed and shared still *another* dimension of "going and doing" in recent days—stopping what we're doing and sitting still. Not the "sitting still" of paralyzed fear, dazed stupor, or sheer denial, but a stopping and sitting to honor and treasure rich resources no violent attack can ever destroy—good deeds done, lives of grace lived—unrepentant lanterns, shining in a dark world.

But "stopping and sitting still" has meant something else for us, I think: A deliberate determination to pause and reflect, before moving on. Do you hear it coming—the question again, *What are we going to do now?* It *is* a time to sit and be still, so that the question can work its way down to who we deeply are, and who we wish to become.

We are told we need closure, so we can begin to put our lives back together and move forward. In some ways, surely, we do need such closure. But there are significant respects in which closure on the recent tragic events (as they are already being tagged) is as inappropriate as it is impossible. Even if a return to business as usual were an available option—which, of course, it is not—few of us would want to go there. Too much has been de-centered, too much is up for grabs, too much is at stake. *What are we going to do now?*

But how can we explore the abyss of that question, if all we have to listen to are the sounds of our own voices, reverberating in the echo chambers of our own minds? If all we have to draw upon are words pouring forth from the media—shrill, strident words demanding our hearing? Perhaps there are other voices that might be invited to join us in the questioning journey. Voices of those, themselves, pushed beyond the breaking point by senseless suffering brought about by violence, terrorism, cruelty. Voices of those we call "people of faith." Voices that might not tell us "just what we wanted to hear." But voices that might help us hear what we need to *do*.

Speak to us, elder sisters and brothers! We have not been, most of us, in a place like this before. Speak to us. We have need of your company, need of your wisdom.

And listening, as we have today, to the voices of a song writer, a poet-prophet, a subversive teacher, and a wide-eyed visionary, here is something we do *not* hear: an executive order—"Now Hear This!" (to which the answer can only be: "Yes, sir. Whatever you say, sir!"). Neither do we hear empty, pious platitudes: "Just trust God; it's gonna be all right." No, what we hear are strange words—words *quiet* and *wild*.

The Lord is my light and my salvation, *whom then shall I fear? One thing I seek—to dwell in the house of the Lord all the days of my life.* Not an escape from chaos, a cozy cave in which to ride out the storm, but "the house of the Lord," a dwelling place, a living space, an energy center for a journey through hell. *Show me your way, O Lord*, the songwriter sings. *Because I do have enemies; Oh God, lead me on a level path.*

Where will that level path lead us? Another voice, the voice of a poet-prophet offers an answer. The level path will lead us: *To bring good news to the oppressed. To bind up the brokenhearted. To proclaim liberty to captives*—not only to prison inmates, but also to long-time victims of economic and political oppression. God's level path will lead us, the poet-prophet suggests, to counter works of terror with a curious vengeance—the proclamation of God's Radical Peace. *To comfort mourners, to rebuild ruined cities*—not just to rebuild towers from rubble, but to dig through, as Isaiah says, "the devastation of many generations"—all that fuels the hatred in acts of terrorism and violence.

Hold it! Time out! Wait a minute, we protest spontaneously. We are in no position to do that!

"*Indeed you are,*" cuts in the voice of the subversive-teacher. *Blessed are the poor in spirit, those who mourn. Blessed are the meek (those who don't have arrogant answers at the tips of their tongues). Blessed are those who want righteous justice (fair distribution, not quick retribution)—blessed are those who want righteousness so badly they can all but taste it. Those who long for justice so deeply, it feels like the pangs of a stomach that hasn't had food for days, like a dehydrated body, desperate for water.*

*Blessed are those who show mercy—regardless. Blessed are those who work for peace—*whatever it costs. *Bless-ed,* not "blessed" the way the President's press secretary used the word recently: "The citizens of our country have a blessed life," which is no longer true in quite the way it was when he said it! But blessed are *we.* You and I are in the best possible place, the most strategic position, to realize the Reign of God, a Commonwealth more real than anything else around.

And then, if that's not overload enough, here comes the word that is really wild, prefaced by a sight too good *not* to be true. A new heaven and new earth, free from horror and carnage, a new city coming down from God, coming down to connect with the "reaching up" work of mourners, mercy messengers, peacemakers. A new city, proving once and for all, that "heaven" has nothing to do with "pie in the sky by and by."

But wait, that isn't all. The word comes once again: *See—the home of God is among mortals. See—God dwells among human beings. God will be with them, as they belong to God.*

And, oh look! Do you see that? God wiping every tear, one by one, from every weeping human eye! Let's take a deep breath, so we can take all this in: wiping tears, *not* saying, "Stop that crying!" But wiping tears from eyes blinded by pain, and grief, and rage. Wiping and wiping, tear after tear, for as long as it takes, for as many who will, so that all can turn with fresh eyes, and behold God's new city. *Behold! I am making all things new!* That's what God says, as God wipes away tears. That is a closure worth having! And that is the *only* closure with a chance in the world, because it is a closure that opens toward utterly new life.

Impractical? It all depends on how you define the word. Frankly, in these voices, *I* hear a clear sense of direction. A marching order I can salute, freely and gladly, with all that I am and all that I do. What I am hearing is this: When my fingers touch the tears of inconsolable suffering, then my fingers are in touch with the finger of God. And if the only way my fingers find to dry the tears of some, is to do what makes others weep, well, it is just possible that I will hear a firm, quiet voice saying: *See here! I am busy drying tears! It is not necessary to bring tears in order to dry tears. On this one—either you are with me or you are not.*

Oh, my God! What are we going to do now?
O dear God! Please help us do what we *need* to do now.

David J. Schlafer is coeditor of this volume.

An earlier form of this sermon appeared in The Journal of the English College of Preachers *112 (January 2002), 7-12.*

PREACHING PAUL

Preaching from the Pauline Epistles: Problems and Possibilities

A. Katherine Grieb

But how are they to call upon one in whom they have not believed? And how are they to believe in one of whom they have never heard? And how are they to hear without someone to proclaim him? And how are they to proclaim him unless they are sent? (Romans 10:14-15a)

I WANT TO URGE a return to the practice of preaching from the letters of Paul, the Church's first theologian and one of its most brilliant thinkers. It is easier to preach on a ready-made story: a parable Jesus tells, a pericope about him from the Gospels, or one of the great narratives of the Old Testament. But I hope to challenge the coming generation of preachers to recover the narrative and parabolic aspects of Pauline theology for a Church that desperately needs to hear his gospel today.

In the Collect for a Theologian (BCP, 248–249), we pray "that the Church may never be destitute of such gifts" as were given to Paul, yet we hardly ever use these gifts in our preaching and teaching in the parish. Why is it so rare to hear a powerful sermon from the Pauline epistles? David Letterman style, I have the top ten reasons:

10. *Because we are expected to preach on the Gospel.* The liturgy and the lectionary set it up that way. Old Testament Lessons and Psalms are chosen to complement the Gospel—the liturgical climax of the lessons.

9. *Because the lectionary tends to isolate epistles except on feast and fast days.* Epistles are generally read through, without link to the Gospel. Preachers who work thematically, as the lectionary encourages, seldom use epistles.

8. *Because many parishes don't read all the lessons, and the epistle is the first to go.* Some parishes read *only* the Gospel, virtually insuring continuing biblical illiteracy.

7. *Because nobody understands Paul's epistles; they're too complicated and abstract.* We might add: and unfamiliar. It's easier to listen closely to something you've heard before.

6. *Because Paul's epistles aren't stories or parables but pieces of an argument.* Gospel pericopes are nicely bounded; it's hard to know where sustained arguments start or stop.

5. *Because, since the epistles assigned are pieces in an argument, we're always coming in on the middle of things.* To get Paul's point, hearers need to know where we are in the argument and what precedes it. Sometimes hearers weren't present last week; usually they can't remember the argument even if they were. Often they aren't listening attentively this week, either, since they're not expecting a sermon on the epistle.

4. *Because Paul's argument often depends on unfamiliar Old Testament quotations.* We rarely hear sermons on the Old Testament either.

3. *Because Paul is perceived as a sexist male chauvinist pig, homophobic, and someone who supported slavery, so nobody in the postmodern world wants to hear from him.* We'll only touch on that one here; but for the record: Paul has gotten a bum rap.

2. *Because Paul was an apocalyptic theologian and Anglicans don't do apocalyptic.* Really? Just because Marcus Borg and the Jesus Seminar don't think Jesus and Paul shared an apocalyptic worldview doesn't mean *you* can't notice the persistent eschatology and strong dualism that characterize the Gospels, Paul's letters, and most of the New Testament.

The most important reason? 1. *Because it demands more of the preacher.* Preaching from the epistles is too much work—not worth the time and trouble.

So the question: Will *we* accept the challenge of preaching Paul? Or will there be yet another generation of God's people left "destitute of these gifts"?

Why a Hermeneutic of Retrieval Is Needed for Paul

From the formation of the New Testament canon onward, it has been difficult to preach Paul. The ecclesiastical priority of the Gospels is shown by their placement. Then comes the Acts of the Apostles, the second half of Luke's grand narrative about Jesus Christ and his Church. Roughly the first half of Acts focuses on the apostle Peter, and, while Luke carefully never refers to Paul as an apostle, the second half of Acts is dominated by Paul. We hear the speeches Luke has crafted for him as we read Luke's powerful account of his missionary journeys and legal defenses all the way to Rome. Paul's letters follow the book of Acts. This means that before we hear a word from Paul himself, we have already been programmed to read Paul in a particular way by Luke's dramatic narrative. Many Christians think they can "get" Paul without actually reading his letters, which are never referred to in Acts.

The Pauline epistles themselves are ordered by length, with Romans first and Philemon last. But the non-Pauline letters attributed to Paul by later copyists (Colossians, Ephesians, and the so-called Pastoral Epistles) are included among letters Paul actually wrote. Because the Pastorals (1 and 2 Timothy and Titus) are short, they appear toward the end of the combined letters, forming (with Philemon) a block of "prison epistles." This encourages readers to think of the much more conservative Pastorals as the end result of Paul's theology—the work of the elderly Paul in prison. Thus, Paul's letters are bracketed by Acts and the Pastorals (both of which are later, more conservative construals of Pauline theology), with other non-Pauline letters (Colossians and Ephesians, also later, more conservative developments of Paul's theology) mixed in. These canonical "givens" make it difficult to recover Paul's own theology, minimizing its controversial features, disabling its explosive gospel.

The canonical framing of Paul is compounded liturgically by the custom of many readers who announce: "A Reading from Paul's Letter to the Ephesians," or "In this lesson, we hear Paul's speech to the Ephesian elders," as if these words, attributed to Paul by later writers, were Paul's own. The Church calendar and the lectionary assist the process of obscuring "the historical Paul" and his dynamic theology of the cross. Even on the Feast of the Conversion of Paul (January 25), we hear the Lukan Paul's account of his conversion to King Agrippa (Acts 26:9-21), Paul's own account of his conversion (Galatians 1:11-24), and a summary of the hardships that await disciples of Jesus (Matthew 10:16-22 —designed to match the account in Acts), but none of Paul's own theology! We have the shell, but none of the contents. We know he *was* converted, but to *what*? We never hear a word of the vision that surges through Paul's letters.

This is no accident. Paul was too hot to handle. He was a problem for the early Church, someone who needed to be domesticated like a wild horse or isolated like a contagious disease. Paul's controversial theology didn't fit into the way the Church was going, which was increasingly establishment and acculturated. Already in the second and third centuries, when the canonical process had begun, but well before it was officially completed, much of the Church was embracing the imperial theology of Ephesians and was well on its way to becoming the official church of the empire, which finally happened under Constantine in the fourth century.

Whatever those early accommodationists thought of Paul, we need to recover his theology today. The Constantinian era is over. We no longer live in a "Christian culture" (if we ever did). We live in a world largely indifferent to the Church. In some places, the culture is passively hostile (condescending and contemptuous). In other places, it actively persecutes the gospel and the Church that preaches it. In other words, we live in a culture much like Paul's world.

Episcopalians especially need to recover Paul. In a recent Gallup poll, people were asked for their opinions of various church denominations. Most people interviewed had "no opinion" about Episcopalians. That ought to worry us! Not because we aren't getting our market share of pledges, but because we aren't doing our share of proclaiming the gospel!

We need Paul to help us preach the gospel in a culture that rejects what it *thinks* Christianity is (which is *not* Christianity). We need Paul to challenge their preconceptions. More important, we need Paul *within* our churches to help reform them according to the gospel, so that we can be credible witnesses to a world that is confused, frightened, and in trouble. It's time to get over whatever threatens us about "evangelism," and to become available to God's mission again, as preachers of God's saving love for the world that so badly needs it.

Why do we need Paul? Paul, like Mark and the author of Hebrews after him, preached a theology of the cross. He preached Christ crucified and raised from the dead. Paul was the first Christian theologian whose writings we have. He may have coined the word "gospel" in the Christian sense; at any rate, he taught us the gospel of Jesus Christ in powerful and challenging words. Paul was an apocalyptic visionary, a change agent who insisted upon a Church conformed to the mind of Christ. Paul was a pastor; he was not afraid to deal with real issues in real churches with real conflicts. He spent the better part of his career working for church unity in situations where congregations tended to splinter and fight. *Do we need Paul or what!*

But how, practically speaking, can we preach him? I want to focus on two common traps in preaching from Paul's letters, and suggest two alternative preaching strategies. *First,* I will focus on the trap of thinking we have to preach Paul's theology as a series of abstract doctrinal propositions, and suggest we adopt a narrative approach instead. *Second*, I will focus on the trap of thinking we have to preach Paul's ethics, his applied theology, as a series of ethical injunctions, and suggest the alternative strategy of describing a vision of the gospel so powerfully that people will long to embrace it.

What's Deadly: Preaching Paul's Theology as a Series of Propositions about Dogmatic Fundamentals

It was Melanchthon, Luther's colleague, who told us Paul's Letter to the Romans was "a compendium of Christian doctrine": Original Sin, Justification by Faith, Predestination, etc. Romans was then used as the standard analysis model for a Pauline letter: part one—theological, doctrinal exposition; part two—ethical injunction, exhortation. Older preaching manuals on the epistles recommend taking a chunk of Paul's argument, deriving its points of doctrine (if it's in the first part of the letter) or points of ethical exhortation (if it's in the second half), then listing those points for the congregation in a series of *dogmatic propositions* to be *digested and believed*, or *ethical injunctions* to be *absorbed and obeyed*. New Testament professors follow this pattern when lecturing on Pauline epistles, usually listing theological points distilled from the epistle for students to memorize and reiterate on the exam. The students come away with "nuggets" of Pauline theology.

Admittedly, in the eighteenth century Jonathan Edwards preached propositions of doctrine (reading for hours from his manuscript, never raising his eyes), and through him the Holy Spirit started a revival that fired the entire Atlantic seaboard! Yet it is well to note *how* he did it. Edwards' sermons are full of visual images. He crafted his words to engage the senses, to invoke the affections (emotions), and to rekindle experienced memories of God's faithfulness. Since then, congregational listening skills and preaching styles have changed. Not many today "stay tuned" for long didactic sermons of doctrinal exposition.

It is puzzling, then, that as recently as 1992, in the *Handbook of Contemporary Preaching* (Nashville, Tenn.: Broadman Press), Scott Hafemann, a prominent New Testament scholar, recommended listing propositions as the preferred strategy for "preaching in the epistles." He included the Pauline epistles, though, significantly, his *examples* are from 2 Peter and the Pastorals, where it could conceivably work. It doesn't work for Paul. Remember that the Pastorals, 2 Peter and Jude, Ephesians, and probably Colossians were written by second- or third-generation Christians living in a world quite different from that of Paul's missionary adventures. They were eager to consolidate doctrine, shore up orthodoxy against challenges, guard the deposit of the faith, tighten up the rules about who could be church leaders, and order Christian households to conform to the culture. In contrast to other early Christian writings of the same period (e.g., the Revelation to John, perhaps the Gospel of John), these authors meant to pin things down and tie things up for a Church that, even at the end of the first century, was planning to be there for the long haul and seeking to accommodate itself to the empire. It is probably simplistic to say even of these later writers that they understood the gospel merely as a series of propositions to be believed and defended, though it can be argued. It cannot possibly be said of Paul.

What's Lifegiving: Recovering the Narrative Substructure of Paul's Letters for Preaching the Gospel Today

Because Paul was a pastor, he cared about people and the stories of their lives. As pastors and preachers we can learn to see people as the subjects of their stories, actors in narratives central to their lives. We may be able to help them locate their stories in the larger story of what God has done in Jesus Christ. We can assist each other to see that great story more clearly by telling the small pieces of it that we know in our own lives. Our preaching will then become—more Pauline!

Paul pastored people by telling them God's story in ways they could ascertain connections between their own stories and what God had done and was doing. When reading Paul's letters, we need to read Paul not as a text but as someone with a story to tell. We need to be good listeners of Paul, to note his manner of presentation, his development of plot and characters, his particular emphases. If Paul is right, this is not just *a* story, but *the* story: the gospel of God, which is "the power of God for salvation" (Romans 1:16).

Instead of thinking in abstracted propositions, we might approach preaching Paul in terms of narrative, the way we would prepare for a sermon on a parable or an episode in the Gospels or Acts. There are at least six strategies for retrieving the narrative substructure of a Pauline epistle: (1) map the story line of the argument; (2) identify the autobiographical sections (the story of Paul and the congregation to which he is writing); (3) locate compressed versions of the gospel story summarized in liturgical and creedal fragments; (4) retrieve Old Testament narratives assumed by Paul and his churches; (5) think typologically, especially where Paul signals that he is relating two narratives typically; (6) work analogically using stories of the present day.

(1) *Map the argument as story.* Let's take the hardest case, Romans, the so-called "compendium of Christian doctrine." Our task is to notice

that Paul has structured his argument in more or less tightly interwoven sections that are based on a series of stories contained in the larger story of what God has done and is doing in Jesus Christ. This story includes all humanity (and even all creation) but is especially about Israel, God's chosen means of redeeming humanity. Because of the death and Resurrection of Jesus Christ, which has inaugurated God's new creation ("newness of life" Romans 6:4), it is also a story about Paul's Gentile churches, which, he insists, are now a part of Israel through the mercies of God. The narrative logic of Paul's theology in Romans might be "mapped" like this:

I. The story of what God has done in the death and resurrection of Jesus Christ
   A. For all of humanity, which was in bondage to Sin and Death
      1. This happened through the fall of Adam, whose disobedience was the opposite of the faithfulness of Jesus Christ (5:12-14)
      2. But God called Abraham, whose faithfulness anticipated the faithfulness of Jesus Christ (4:18-22)
      3. These actions of our ancient ancestors have important implications for those of us "in Jesus Christ" as well (5:15-21; 4:1, 10-12, 23-25)
   B. For the creation itself, which was enslaved along with the rest of humanity
      1. This also happened through the unfaithfulness of Adam (8:20-22)
      2. But Abraham trusted in God's salvation-creating power over creation in spite of Sin and Death (4:17)
      3. Those "in Jesus Christ," though presently suffering, anticipate, along with creation, the glory about to be revealed (8:18-19)
   C. For Israel, which was supposed to be God's plan for redemption
      1. Israel experienced its own special "fall" in the incident of the golden calf under Moses and is therefore "Adam intensified" through the giving of the Law (7:7-13)
      2. But the promise to Abraham (now fulfilled in Jesus Christ) did not come through the Law (4:13)
      3. So Abraham is the key ancestor of those who are circumcised (4:12)
      4. Those "in Jesus Christ" (the seed of Abraham) are rescued from Sin and Death and receive the inheritance promised to Abraham and to his seed (3:21, 4:13, 9:29)

D. For Paul's Gentile churches, which are now part of Israel
   1. And therefore share the whole history of the fall, both Adam and the golden calf
   2. But are also rightful descendants of Abraham, the ancestor of those who trust God without being circumcised (4:11)
   3. Those "in Jesus Christ," whether Jew or Greek, are one, as God is one (3:29-31)
E. The heart of the story: Jesus Christ's "obedience of faith" leading to his death on the cross and God's faithfulness ("righteousness") in raising him from the dead (Romans 3:21-31)
   1. Which undoes the disobedience of Adam "by much more" (5:15-21)
   2. Which links us to the promise given to faithful Abraham and to his seed (4:13, 16)
   3. Those "in Jesus Christ" are called to imitate his faithfulness (1:5, 16:26). *Paul's special call is to win "obedience of faith" from the Gentiles called to believe in Jesus Christ*

II. The story of what God is presently doing and about to do in the newness of resurrection life inaugurated in Jesus Christ
A. For all of humanity:
   1. God invites us to hope in God's continuing mercies as we face the wrath to come
   2. Since Christ died for us while we were sinners (reconciled us to God as enemies), surely we will be saved by his life (resurrection), which is proof that God keeps promises (5:6-11).
   3. Nothing will be able to separate us from the love of God in Christ Jesus (8:39)
B. For the whole creation:
   1. Creation still groans in labor pains waiting for the revealing of God's children, longing to be set free from its slavery to corruption and to obtain the freedom of God's children
   2. We ourselves groan with creation, waiting in hope for adoption, the redemption of our bodies.
   3. God's Spirit also groans, interceding for the saints according to God (8:20-27)
C. For Israel, God's chosen people:
   What is God doing here, allowing the Gentiles to respond in faith while Israel, God's own people, refuses its Messiah (9-11)? *This is the itch that drives Paul's scratch in the whole epistle. His anguished outworking of God's election, Israel's unbelief, Gentile arrogance, and his own apostleship.*

D. For Paul's Gentile churches (composed of Jews and Gentiles):
  1. All are one in Jesus Christ because God is One (3:29-31)
  2. Gentile Christians need to remember their great debt to Israel, the people of the Messiah (11:13-32)

E. The heart of the appeal:
  1. Welcome those with whom you disagree because God has welcomed them (14:1-4)
  2. Welcome one another as Christ has welcomed you (15:1-7)
  3. Imitate the faithfulness of Jesus Christ in two ways:
    a. internally in your life together (you should quit fighting)
    b. externally, in your support of Paul's mission to Gentiles in Spain (15:1-13, 23-24)

The second part of our outline is predictably less clear. Paul can say a lot more about what God has done than about what God will do. Moreover, since Paul's argument in Romans is essentially a defense of God's covenant righteousness, both to Israel and to the Gentiles, he needs to argue from the record of God's actions in Israel's Scriptures. In order to demonstrate God's fidelity to Israel in the present context of the Gentile mission, Paul appeals from God's *modus operandi* in the past to argue for trusting God in the present and future. In short, Paul tells the story of God's righteousness throughout his epistle to the Romans. The same strategy of recovering the story within the argument itself could be applied to Galatians, Philippians, and the rest of Paul's epistles.

(2) *Identify autobiographical sections.* Once we have achieved an overview of the storied structure in which Paul's argument is framed, we can begin to uncover the narrative substructure beneath particular sections of the argument. Our task here is to learn to recognize the story hidden beneath Paul's words. The easiest place to do this is where Paul speaks in the first person, usually at the beginning or the end of the letter. Here he often speaks autobiographically as he writes of his desire to visit the congregation and shares his travel plans with them.

At the beginning of his letter to the Romans, Paul describes himself as "Paul, a slave of Jesus Christ, called apostle, set apart for the gospel of God." This gospel of God "was promised in advance by God through the prophets in the Holy Scriptures." He means, of course, Israel's prophets in the Holy Scriptures of Israel. These Scriptures are "about God's Son." Paul elaborates: the Scriptures are about God's Son, "who was descended from David according to the flesh and was declared Son of God in power according to the Spirit of holiness by resurrection from the dead." God's Son is "Jesus Christ our Lord," through whom Paul has been commissioned "to bring about the obedience of faith" among the nations, the Gentiles, including some of you Romans who are Gentiles, "called to belong to Jesus Christ."

Notice that everything Paul has said (in this one very long sentence in Greek) is in apposition to his name. He is describing himself. The standard beginning of a Greek letter goes: Sender (Paul) to the Receiver (the church in Rome) Greetings! But so far, this long convoluted sentence only modifies Paul. In a moment, he will address them as "God's beloved in Rome, who are called to be saints" and he will send them greetings: "Grace to you and peace from God our Father and the Lord Jesus Christ." In the meantime, Paul cannot introduce himself without alluding to a story—not just *any* story, but *the* story so central to Paul's life that it is what makes him "Paul."

The pattern is even more striking in Galatians, where the first two chapters form a paradigmatic autobiography, designed to encourage the Galatians to stand fast (as Paul defended the gospel at Antioch) and to throw out rival missionaries who were urging circumcision (as Paul had triumphed over the false brothers attempting to circumcise Titus). Similarly, in Philippians 3:4b-14, Paul tells his own story, along with that of his co-workers Timothy and Epaphroditus (2:19-30), to illustrate what the Christ-pattern described in the quoted hymn (2:6-11) looks like in action. Again, in 2 Corinthians 12:2-10, Paul tells (in cryptic fashion) a story involving both secret visions (heavenly revelations) and some embarrassing physical weakness (his thorn in the flesh) to suggest the complex relationship between power and weakness that lies at the heart of his gospel. These autobiographical narratives form an integral part of Paul's argument, for the imitation of Christ or for the defense of the gospel.

At the endings of Paul's letters, there are often first-person statements that reveal another narratival layer in the epistles: the story of Paul's relationship with the congregation he is addressing. In Romans, as in Philemon, the conclusion of the argument is integrally linked with the expressed hope to visit the recipients of the letter. In the conflicted letter of Galatians, on the other hand, two intensely personal recollections of the shared past history of Paul and the Galatians are built right into the argument (3:1-5 and 4:12-20) and the end of the letter refers to yet another story (that of Paul's sufferings for Christ) designed to lend weight to his appeal to them to defend the gospel (6:17).

(3) *Locate (and unpack) compressed versions of the gospel story.* The narrative of what God has done in Jesus Christ is often summarized in liturgical or creedal fragments quoted by Paul at critical points of his argument. Paul is probably quoting such traditional material in the first verses of Romans described above. The clearest examples are Paul's use of the Christ hymn in Philippians 2:6-11 and his use of eucharistic and resurrection traditions in 1 Corinthians (11:23-26, 15:3-11) to allude to narratives of the Last Supper and the Easter appearances preserved in the (later) gospels. But even in Romans, Paul's most "doctrinal" epistle, and even in its most doctrinally dense section (3:21-26), narrative accounts of God's faithfulness in Jesus Christ are hidden beneath his words. To retrieve them, we must unpack the powerful metaphors Paul uses to speak of what God has done through the faithfulness of Jesus Christ.

Paul describes the death and resurrection of Jesus, God's saving act that has inaugurated the new creation and freed humanity from the clutches of Sin and Death, in compact, almost formulaic terms. Within these few verses (3:21-26) Paul speaks of *redemption* (the buying back of family members out of debt slavery), *justification* (the rescue of defendants on death row), and *atonement* (the forgiveness of sins through liturgical sacrifice in the Holy of Holies). In other words, each of these compressed metaphors alludes to a larger story well known to Paul's original hearers.

It is as if Paul gave us only the file name we needed to call up the entire document. It is as if he had merely mentioned Desmond Tutu, knowing that hearers would call up the whole story of the long brave struggle against apartheid in South Africa, the long list of martyrs like Stephen Biko, the imprisonment of Nelson Mandela, and the work of the Truth and Reconciliation Commission. The name Desmond Tutu functions by metonymy to refer to the entire story, well known by the Church today. Two centuries from now, the reference "Desmond Tutu" would need explaining. The story could not simply be alluded to; its most basic features would have to be retold. In the same way, these extended metaphors (submerged parables), compressed by Paul into a few words, need to be unpacked and explained for congregations today, for whom the words "redemption," "justification," and "atonement" no longer conjure up the great stories of Israel's life with God that Paul and his hearers remembered.

(4) *Retrieve the Old Testament history assumed by Paul.* Throughout his longer letters, Paul makes extensive use of narratives from the Old

Testament, retelling them creatively for his purposes, or alluding to them in order to advance his argument. In 1 Corinthians 10, Paul summarizes the story of Israel in the wilderness (read christologically and sacramentally) to warn his congregation about the dangers of idolatry. In 2 Corinthians 3, Paul alludes to the story of Moses on Mount Sinai receiving the Law to talk about the greater glory of the new covenant in Jesus Christ. The argument in Galatians draws upon the story of Abraham, Sarah, and Hagar—Paul calls it an "allegory" (4:24)—to contrast the theology of the rival missionaries with Paul's own gospel. And from start to finish, Romans alludes to Old Testament narratives, from the fall of Adam to the children of the prophet Hosea, to describe God's covenant faithfulness. For a fuller account, see my *The Story of Romans: A Narrative Defense of God's Righteousness* (Louisville, Ky.: Westminster John Knox Press, 2002). For an insightful study of Paul's use of Scripture throughout his letters, see Richard Hays' *Echoes of Scripture in the Letters of Paul* (New Haven, Conn.: Yale University Press, 1989).

(5) Expand typological references in the argument. Sometimes Paul signals his readers directly that he is relying on typological connections between characters, events, or situations in the submerged narrative and his own argument. In the passage from 1 Corinthians 10 about Israel's idolatry in the wilderness, Paul tells us "these things happened typically" (literally "as types of us") so that we (Paul's churches, then later readers) could learn from their experience not to desire evil as they did (10:6). He explains again (10:11): "These things happened to them typically and they were written down for our instruction, upon whom the ends of the ages have come." Similarly, in Romans 5:14 Paul describes Adam as "a type of the one who was to come" (Jesus Christ). The relationship between Jesus Christ and Adam is one of *negative* typology— Paul stresses not their similarity, but their difference. Adam's disobedience, through which Sin and Death entered the world, is the opposite of Christ's obedience, which has won for us eternal life. Abraham in Romans 4, on the other hand, is an example of *positive* typology: the faithfulness of Abraham points ahead to the faithfulness of Jesus Christ, just as the obedience of faith that Paul seeks to win from Gentiles looks back to and reflects the faithfulness of Jesus Christ. Sometimes the typological relationship is complex, as in the Moses typology of 2 Corinthians 3, neither exactly positive or negative, neither entirely christological or ecclesiological. Paul's biblical allusiveness is playful, poetic, and understated. He requires considerable work from his readers—and his expositors! By mentioning the word "type" (or

"allegory") or using typology without mentioning it, Paul encourages his hearers to recover the ancient story (of Israel, Adam, Abraham and Sarah, Moses) and compare it with the story of Jesus Christ (Romans 5) or the story of Paul's churches (Galatians 4, 1 Corinthians 10) or both (Romans 4, 2 Corinthians 3).

Except in the few places where Paul expressly retells the older story, none of this narrative web appears on the surface—it's all substructure. Paul alludes to stories that are the foundation of his argument. We who preach Romans 4 or 2 Corinthians 3 need to show our congregations how Paul's typology works so that they can follow the argument, otherwise they'll never get it, never see what's going on, hear Paul's theology, or understand Paul's vision for the Church.

(6) *Work with contemporary analogies.* The strategy for uncovering the narrative substructure of the Pauline epistles is already familiar to preachers working with narratives like parables or episodes from the Gospels. To communicate what is at stake, preachers tell a similar or opposite story from another time and place, often from a contemporary setting. The congregation can then work backwards from the characters, plot, or situation of the second story to hear the biblical narrative with new ears. (Technically, this sort of analogy is another instance of typology.) Of course, there are homiletical dangers in using this approach: the new story can be so dramatic or be told so powerfully that it eclipses the biblical one; the new story can be so trivial that it cheapens the biblical narrative by comparison; the connections may be too strained for the hearers to put them together. But, well done, this preaching strategy unveils the narrative substructure supporting even a single sentence, such as "My grace is sufficient for you, for power is made perfect in weakness."

When preaching from the Pauline epistles, then, try communicating Paul's theology through stories within, implied, or alluded to *in* the text, or designed to *complement* the text. Replace the strategy of abstracting doctrinal propositions from the letters with uncovering narrative accounts of God's faithfulness in Jesus Christ. Reading through Paul's densely constructed arguments, watch for clues that signal a narrative hidden within or underneath.

Paul's Apocalyptic Ethics and the Task of Preaching for Conversion

Now I want to focus on the application sections of Paul's letters (which, incidentally, are not always found in the second half: Paul's theology and his ethics are tightly interwoven throughout his letters). Here I suggest that instead of listing a series of ethical injunctions abstracted from the text, it would be both more life giving and more faithful to Paul to engage hearers in parable mode—to describe a moral vision of God's new creation in Jesus Christ, then to invite hearers into living that.

Paul wrote his epistles because he was trying to hold his churches together amid the stresses and strains that tended to divide them from each other and to separate them from himself. When we're dealing with Pauline epistles, it helps to remember we're reading someone else's mail. These letters were saved because the community to whom they were written valued them well beyond the time of the situation that occasioned them. Presumably at some later time, they were circulated to other churches that also found them helpful. Eventually they found their way onto canonical lists and into the collection of early Christian writings that later became the New Testament. As New Testament scholar Leander Keck once remarked, "The New Testament is something that happened to these writings." Paul had no idea his letters to his struggling missions would be gathered and published in a book to be studied by people thousands of years later. He wasn't writing for posterity: he didn't think there was going to *be* a posterity! But here we are, and when we read these letters, we notice Paul's congregations struggled with many of the issues we face. I am constantly grateful to those early Christians who, when commanded to hand over their sacred writings, refused to do so, willing to become martyrs if necessary so that "the truth of the gospel" in these texts might be preserved for us.

It also helps to remember that these letters were understood as a substitute for the personal presence of the apostle who could not come to the church in person, but who sent his words to them. As J. Louis Martyn reminds us, Paul's letters would have been "performed" (enacted, embodied, incarnated if you will) by someone coached by Paul about how to present the letter rhetorically. Paul seems to have expected his hearers to experience both his own presence with them and the gospel of God spoken in his words through the power of God's Spirit. Clearly, Paul had a strong doctrine of the Holy Spirit. The letters he wrote were not only to serve as a reminder of his relationship in Christ to the congregation. He seems to have believed that God through his words could connect him with the congregation from which he was far distant. He trusted the Holy Spirit to re-preach the gospel in the very event of reading his letter, so that its recipients would again experience the power of God for salvation, the truth of the gospel, just as they had at the beginning, when they had first heard the good news of Jesus Christ (Martyn, *Galatians*, New York: Doubleday, 1997, 21–23). In a sense, then, Paul's letters are already sermons: reminders to his churches of his earlier preaching, filled with allusions to stories, hymns, and experiences of God they had previously shared with him. It is not a matter of homiletical insignificance, therefore, how contemporary preachers undertake the task of "preaching like Paul."

What's Deadly: Preaching Paul as a Series of Ethical Injunctions

There's no question that Paul has strong opinions about issues in church community life and doesn't mind giving his opinion when asked—or even when not asked. But it doesn't work to read Paul's ethical injunctions out of the verses of his letters as if he spoke to all situations and to all times equally. Often the Word of God comes to us in parables that require us to look at ourselves and our world differently. The preacher has some discerning to do, to make the connections, to find the appropriate analogies, and to discard the false clarity that sometimes occurs when people want to read ethics right off the page. "God said it, I believe it, that settles it" may be the slogan of some Christians, but it leads to sermons that are both unkind and ungodly. As Richard Hays has commented, "Bumper sticker ethics simply won't do."

Neither will the appeal to "decision" that has funded the existentialist reading of Paul. "I have decided to follow Jesus" is a fine hymn, but it is not Paul's. We may sing it along with Matthew and James; but Paul is singing "Amazing grace . . . that saved a wretch like me." If we buy into the doctrine of "decision," then with a little assistance from God, people can *choose*: between law and gospel (Luther); between life and death (Deuteronomy, Leviticus). For Paul, that's bad news: if we, enslaved to Sin and Death, do the choosing, we will get it wrong: God's ways are not our ways; God's thoughts are not our thoughts. We do not willingly choose the cross. The cross chooses us. What looks and feels like death brings life in God.

How, then, can the contemporary preacher appropriately honor Paul's attempt to embody "the truth of the gospel" in his concern to address the serious moral concerns confronting the congregations to which he was speaking? How can preachers *translate* such embodiment *dynamically* for the moral concerns of today? A brief excursus on imagination and evangelism will be helpful in making such a bridge.

"Not That There Is Another Gospel, But There Are Some Who Trouble You"

Walter Brueggemann, in *Biblical Perspectives on Evangelism: Living in a Three-Storied Universe⁻* (Nashville: Tenn.: Abingdon, 1993), describes the importance of imagination in the task of evangelism. He says:

> [T]he decisive clues for our practice of evangelism are found in the drama and dynamic transaction of the biblical text itself . . . I assume that the biblical text is not a handbook for morality or doctrine as it is often regarded, nor on the other hand, is it an historical record, as many are wont to take it. Rather the biblical text is the articulation of imaginative models of reality in which "text-users," i.e., readers in church and synagogue, are invited to participate. (page 8)

The evangelical church must know its stories and be able to tell them with power, because "evangelism means inviting people into these stories as the definitional story of our life, and thereby authorizing people to give up, abandon, and renounce other stories that have shaped their lives in false and distorting ways." Story telling is not a neutral activity. None of us lives in a world without stories, but rather we live in a world with many competing stories. Our imaginations are saturated with stories to which we have made trusting (even if unwitting) commitments. Evangelism "is an invitation and summons to 'switch stories,' and therefore to change lives" (page 11).

It is September 2001 as I am revising these lectures for publication, shortly after the terrorist attack that felled the towers of the World Trade Center and branded a flaming gash in the Pentagon. Thousands have been killed or seriously wounded from the hijacking of commercial jetliners (named "United" and "American") for deployment as missiles against the most prominent symbols of United States economic and military superiority. The nation's heart has been broken; its pride wounded. Many U.S. citizens can think only of revenge; the pollsters say that 90 percent of citizens support war—described, of course, as a war of prevention against specific terrorists and their supporters. Again and again we hear how everything has been changed by these events: heightened security measures, fear of economic recession, widespread anxiety.

Yet it is clear that one important thing has not yet been changed: as a nation, we are not yet willing to undertake an examination of conscience, the "searching and fearless moral inventory" that might lead us to confession of sin and acknowledgement of wrongdoing on *our* part toward the poorer nations of the world. As the United States closes ranks, internal voices self-critical of our foreign policy are branded as unpatriotic. While a united Congress grants the president "whatever he needs" in the way of war powers, a convenient distraction is provided by the religious right, as Jerry Falwell and Pat Robertson blame feminists, homosexuals, the ACLU, and others for God's wrath against "America." External allies are pressured for uncritical endorsements and statements of unconditional support for the United States. We are apparently not yet willing to hear the voices of those who question the wisdom of our foreign policies, let alone the voices of those who deeply resent our actions that have destabilized their own governments and economies. In this deafness, we seem to think that only our "enemies" would say that we might in any way have brought this terrible tragedy upon ourselves by our past military and economic policies.

One way preachers can analyze this situation is to call to mind the large repertoire of biblical stories that problematize the theology of empire. Daniel and Revelation warn about the self-delusions of those who think they rule the world; 1 Kings and Jeremiah teach that discernment is required: not all professed prophets speak for the Lord; Amos is warned not to prophesy at Bethel "for it is the king's sanctuary"; Peter and the apostles announce that they must obey God rather than people. Not all biblical texts speak with one voice on any subject, of course. There are plenty of holy war texts and admonitions to be subject to and pray for those in authority. But nowhere in its pages does the Bible recommend uncritical allegiance to anyone but God. Instead it invites discernment from its readers: where are we in the story? What questions does the biblical text raise for us about ourselves and our obedience to God?

We have a story about ourselves that we tell in the United States and it has been told again and again with particular energy since the tragic events of September eleventh: we are "America" (never mind the dozens of other nations in South, Central, and North America who also think of themselves as "Americans") and we are good ("Freedom was attacked today") while our enemies are evil, barbaric, and cowardly. We were completely innocent, but we are not victims; we will grow even more powerful as a result of this attack. We defend order, predictability, and civilization; our enemies are intent upon bringing chaos upon the whole civilized world. Therefore an attack on "America" is an attack on all freedom-loving people everywhere and it will not prevail. God will bless "America."

This is the story that we will tell ourselves as we go to war, but what would it mean to think of the Bible's words as an invitation and summons to *switch stories* and therefore to *change lives?* Could we join with other nations to eradicate terrorism, as we must, by whatever diplomatic and economic means are available to us, and at the same time use this tragic occasion to ask some deeper questions of ourselves and our values, to reexamine the truth of the story we tell ourselves? Can we see any humanity in our enemies? Can we learn to look at the world situation from any other point of view than our own self-interested one? Can we learn to see ourselves as many other nations see us—terrorists in our own right? Can preaching the biblical texts help us to reorient ourselves and see the world from another perspective? The God who speaks through these biblical stories may well be calling us to "switch stories" and change our national life in ways we can hardly imagine.

In another book, *Texts Under Negotiation: The Bible and Postmodern Imagination* (Minneapolis: Fortress, 1993), Brueggemann suggests an important learning about how people change: *not* as a result of getting clarity about doctrine, *nor* in response to a direct moral appeal. People change their hearts and minds when they are given *a new model, construal, or interpretation of reality and are shown how they can fit their own story into this altered way of seeing reality.* So imagination is critical, poetical, and finally ethical: our present situation is the Enlightenment's failure of imagination; therefore, our present task is to fund or authorize a counterimagination that problematizes the known world. This is in fact what the Bible is already doing: it offers a proposed world that clashes with the presumed world of our culture. Brueggemann's question to the Church is: "Have we enough confidence in the biblical text to let it be our fund for counterimagination?" (page 25).

Paul, as an evangelist in his own day, would have understood perfectly what Brueggemann is talking about: the gospel of God is saving reality, but there are other rival interpretations of reality that God's story must displace. Paul writes to the Galatians that there is no other gospel than the reality of God's gracious power, but, he warns, "there are some who trouble you and who wish to change the gospel of God into its opposite" (Galatians 1:7). Again and again the Bible requires discernment about who is troubling Israel and who is not. Which is the gospel and which is the counterfeit gospel that is being marketed as saving reality when in reality it leads only to death and destruction? Paul *does* have confidence in the biblical text as the source of reality markers for himself and for his congregations. These are God's promises made ahead of time through the prophets of the Holy Scriptures of Israel. As we listen to this gifted evangelist at work, we preachers can learn to listen to the Bible with contemporary ears, to tell the gospel in a visionary mode, and to anticipate imaginative ways of communicating the ethical impact of God's action in Jesus Christ.

What's Lifegiving: The Moral Vision of Paul's Apocalyptic Ethics

The focusing image of new creation is especially important for preaching the Pauline epistles as a whole, not only 2 Corinthians 5 and Galatians 6, where Paul explicitly uses the words "new creation." Following C. H. Dodd's usage in the Gospel of John and elsewhere, we might describe this phrase as a "submerged parable." A parable places two things beside each other for comparison (e.g., "With what can we compare the kingdom of God, or what parable will we use for it? It is like a mustard seed . . ." Mark 4:30-31). In 2 Corinthians 5:17 Paul compares the situation of being in Christ with new creation. We can imagine Paul as he struggles to find words strong enough to convey the radical change that envelopes a person who is brought into the sphere of God's gracious reign in Jesus Christ and as he finally lands on the metaphor of new creation. What other image could convey as strongly how much everything has changed as a result of God's action in the death and resurrection of Jesus Christ?

In Galatians 6:15, Paul uses the phrase to show how very unimportant the issue of circumcision or uncircumcision is in the life of the community to which the world has been crucified by the cross of Christ. What difference could it possibly make in the new creation! Once again, it is the radical nature of the change that is stressed: the difference is unlike anything we have ever seen in this world. The preacher's task is to paint a vivid word picture of the new creation, reminding hearers of God's calling that frees people from enslaving structures of Sin and Death so that they may live to God.

Paul is an apocalyptic theologian. The most important thing to know about apocalyptic theology is "What time is it?" What time is it on God's watch? Never mind what time Caesar says it is (Caesar may not be here tomorrow). Never mind what time it feels like (our feelings can be deceptive). The call is for endurance and wisdom to discern the times: what is the reality and what is the illusion?

With what shall we compare the reign of God? How can we describe the radical disjunction between the old cosmos that is perishing and the new cosmos that has already begun with God's gracious re-creation of the world in the death and resurrection of Jesus Christ? It's a matter of life and death for Paul, both literally (the death of Jesus on the Cross) and metaphorically (in the death of the believer in baptism). If we look at just a few of the analogies, parables, and metaphors Paul uses to describe God's salvation-creating power, we see that he speaks of being "baptized into the death" of Christ, "buried with him" so that "just as Christ was raised from the dead by the glory of the Father, so we too might walk in newness of life" (Romans 6:3-4); he describes getting in step with the Spirit since those who belong to Christ "have crucified the flesh with its passions" (Galatians 5:24-25); and he regards everything he had before he was in Christ as rubbish (dung), not caring that he has suffered the loss of all things for the sake of Christ if only he may "know Christ and the power of his resurrection and the sharing of his sufferings" (Philippians 3:7-11).

Part of the task in framing helpful analogies is to figure out what's at stake for the Church and its members: then and now. We see Paul doing this consistently in the chapters of 1 Corinthians. He shows the church at Corinth that they are not as spiritually mature as they think they are, distances himself from the baptismal charism they think is so important, and refocuses their attention on the cross (1-2). Paul discusses lawsuits among Christian believers, and argues that no matter who wins, everybody loses (6). He tells them concerning idol meat: *Yes, yes, you can eat anything, but look what happens to the community when you exercise your so-called "right," and don't be too sure that there aren't demons associated with that cup which is the symbol of your uncaring self-interested action* (8-10). He criticizes their potluck suppers: *You wealthy, privileged ones get there early and eat all the good food and drink all the wine, so that when the servant class arrives, there's nothing left and no real opportunity for communion* (11). In all of these situations, Paul cares less about who's right or who's wrong in Corinth than about what is happening to the body of Christ there.

The same thing is true in other letters. Once he is able to show the congregation what is at stake in their pastoral situation—often by using an analogy, metaphor, or parable—Paul can offer a new moral vision and invite them to live into it. This is especially evident in Philippians 2-3. Paul is in prison. He is the Nelson Mandela, the Martin Luther King Jr., the Dietrich Bonhoeffer of his day, writing with all the spiritual power and integrity inherent in the "prison letter" genre. Writing to his (apparently) fractious and selfish congregation in Philippi, Paul doesn't yell at them or order them to stop fighting. He certainly doesn't list a string of biblical proof texts about getting along. Instead, first he shows them the vision of the cross of Christ as the model of giving one's life for others; then he lifts up his coworkers Timothy and Epaphroditus as examples of self-giving love; next he tells the story of his conversion and the radical shift from persecuting the Church to participating in the sufferings of Christ; finally, he invites the Philippians to join the party. They are to think more highly of others than of themselves as Jesus did; they are to imitate the courage and dedication of Paul's coworkers; they are to join Paul in running the race (an athletic metaphor, functioning as another submerged parable); what he has given them is an invitation to "switch stories and to change lives."

The same is true in Galatians 2 (the Antioch showdown between Peter and Paul) regarding the question of table fellowship between Jews and Gentiles. It's easy enough to see that segregation here and apartheid in South Africa were and are contraindicated by the gospel of God. What is more difficult to see is a vision of new creation. The preacher's challenge is to show what that looks like on the ground, to describe a Church caring enough about unity in Christ to be able to overcome racial and ethnic divisions, even in the face of intense cultural pressure to conform to the old age.

One of the most remarkable stories of this kind from recent history emerged out of the bloody conflict in Rwanda, where in 1994 members of the Hutu tribe carried out mass murders of the Tutsi tribe. At the town of Ruhanga, fifteen kilometers outside Kigali, a group of 13,500 Christians had gathered for refuge. They were of various denominations: Anglicans, Romans Catholics, Pentecostals, Baptists, and others. According to the account of a witness to the scene, "When the militias came, they ordered the Hutus and Tutsis to separate themselves by tribe. The people refused and declared that they were all one in Christ, and for that they were all killed," gunned down en masse and dumped into group graves. The story is deeply disturbing on one level, but on another level it is a profound witness to the power of the gospel to overcome ethnic division. Paul would have not have encouraged anyone to seek martyrdom—which is always God's decision, not ours—but he probably would have seen these Rwandan martyrs as faithful witnesses to the truth of the gospel he was preaching in Galatians. Having been "crucified with Christ," they preferred to die rather than to deny the grace of God that had made them one in Christ (cited in Hays, "Galatians," *New Interpreter's Bible,* Nashville, Tenn.: Abingdon, 248).

Much of Paul's apocalyptic spirituality depends on the fundamental contrast between what is real and what is illusory. Just as it is critical to know what time it is (new creation!), so it is critical to know who is Lord in the face of rival claims to authority. In the case of Galatians, rival missionaries claim their authority from the Jerusalem Church. They seem to be using exclusion from the Church as a missionary tactic: "They make much of you but for no good purpose; they want to exclude you, so that you may make much of them" (4:17). This behavior continues to be a live option in the Church today: you're not a real Christian unless you do this action, hold that belief, have been to this event, or have visited that holy place. Paul cuts right through all of that: it isn't something *we* do that makes us a real Christian. God does the reality piece; all of this other gamey stuff is only illusion. Framing the vision often means naming its opposite, its counterfeit. The point of telling an apocalyptic vision of God's new creation is to stand the apparent reality of the counterfeit gospel on its head, to problematize "what we all know is true" by describing a reality so real that the known world pales in comparison to it.

This is the task of the preacher of Paul's epistles because it was Paul's own task as he crafted his sermon-letters for the needs of his local congregations: to provide a moral vision of God's new creation so compelling that his hearers would abandon behavior that once made sense to them, because they could now see themselves in a new world that they could never even have imagined before.

Preaching for conversion requires not only trust in God and confidence that the biblical text can indeed fund our descriptions of the counter-world of the reign of God; it also requires the right tools: parable, metaphor, analogy, color, texture, sound, powerful verbal pictures. Recommendation: Replace that list of ethical injunctions abstracted from Paul's epistles with a description of his moral vision: show your listeners the new creation and summon them to live into it! Our culture as a whole and each of us within it are captive to the power of narratives that are inadequate for living our lives in accordance with the truth of the gospel. These counterfeit gospels that promise salvation are deceitful brooks that dry up in times of crisis; shifting sands upon which no house can stand when great winds blow; illusion, not the reality of God's reign. To defeat them, preachers must describe the vision, speak about God's new creation in vivid and compelling metaphors, and send out invitations summoning those who can hear to let themselves be written into the story of God's salvation-creating power. This will often be costly and lonely, which is why, when Jesus invited the rich man (Mark 10 and parallels) to switch stories and change lives, he not only summoned him to give up his possessions, he also promised him a new community: "Come, follow me!"

The retrieval of Paul's voice in the Church is an uphill fight, but one worth fighting. It requires more of preachers than parables or a story about Jesus from the Gospels. We must make Paul's letters available to today's Church: When preaching doctrine, instead of listing propositions, try using a narrative approach. When preaching ethics, instead of listing injunctions and commands, try replacing them with descriptions of Paul's moral vision, showing what the new creation looks like, sounds like, feels like, inviting listeners to the party, summoning them to the banquet. The alternative narratives and counterfeit gospels of the culture around us are not "harmless distractions" as video games are often thought to be; they have real and deadly consequences. Preaching for conversion is sending out invitations to "switch stories and change lives."

A. Katherine Grieb is Associate Professor of New Testament at Virginia Theological Seminary in Alexandria, Virginia.

8

A WORD EMERGING:

The Promise of Performance Studies for Homiletics

Richard Ward
Joanne Buchanan-Brown

ONCE, WHILE TEACHING at the Candler School of Theology at Emory University, I walked by Cannon Chapel and saw a dance troupe getting ready for a rehearsal. First, they carefully laid down a soft surface on top of the chapel's hard wooden floor—a surface firm but springy enough to allow lifts and leaps. Next the dancers themselves moved onto the surface to try it out. Initially they were cautious, making tentative moves. Soon, however, their confidence grew. They began risking bold leaps and turns. Dances started taking shape. Individual dancers became an ensemble. Music flowed through the space, and, in response, the dancers advanced upon and retreated from the surface.

I sat unnoticed in a corner, watching and listening. I became particularly interested in two dancers rehearsing a *pas de deux*. Slowly they approached each other. They embraced. One lifted the other. They started to spin in a carefully choreographed sequence of moves. Occasionally the music and flow of movement would stop as they corrected one another, gave each other instructions, and received coaching from the others. They tried the movement again and again until they were satisfied with it.

The setting turned out to be a good place for reflecting on the practice of preaching. The memory of that event has slowly evolved into a metaphor. Like a dancer in a troupe, the preacher enters into a dynamic collaboration with a variety of partners in order to shape an embodied response to the "music" of God's Spirit. The voices and presences found in texts, tradition, and congregation embrace and lift. They can correct the preacher, but also yield to the correction of the preacher as he or she shapes a word that is faithful to the gospel for our time.

Linking preaching to another expressive art is a familiar ploy among homileticians. Eugene Lowry compares the process and preparation of sermons to jazz.[1] Mary Catherine Hilkert casts the preacher in the role of the sermon's narrator who pulls thoughts, memories, reflections, and interpretations into a satisfying whole.[2] Mike Graves compares preaching to a symphony.[3] Jana Childers and Alec Gilmore both compare preaching to theatre.[4] Why such a proliferation of metaphors drawn from the arts to speak about preaching? Those of us who teach preaching like to make links between preaching and the arts because such links loosen preaching from tight moorings in discursive, rational thought. Comparing preaching to other expressive arts enables us to see sermon preparation as a *creative process*; the act of speaking the sermon as *aesthetic communication*.

"Performance studies" offers ways to understand the aesthetic dimensions of both the preaching event and the preaching preparation process. Here I want to move that idea forward, first, by defining "performance" as an evocative way of describing the spoken sermon, and then by showing how "performance studies" fosters an *oral hermeneutic* for reading and speaking the texts from which we preach.

The Sermon in Performance: Speaking a Lively Word

Performance studies is a discipline arising out of the study of human communication. One of its assumptions is that human beings engage in an ongoing process of giving speech to their thoughts and feelings. To speak is to *act*. Speech is an enactment of thought and motive. Since voices belong to bodies, we can even say that *a spoken word* is *an embodied thought*. It is a *doing* as much as it is *a saying*. The *forms* such speaking and enacting assume are richly varied: from everyday conversation, to poetry and playwriting, through ritual, and even toward ecstatic speech. Some of these forms are framed as art, obeying principles and conventions that a culture deems appropriate for artistic communication. Other forms, elements in human–divine interaction, are deemed sacred or religious.

All human speech and enactment is laden with values and symbolic significance. As I pass a colleague on her way out of the mailroom I say:

---

1. Eugene L. Lowry, "The Narrative Quality of Experience as a Bridge to Preaching," in *Journeys toward Narrative Preaching,* ed. Wayne Bradley Robinson (New York: Pilgrim Press, 1990), 70.

2. Mary Catherine Hilkert, *Naming Grace: Preaching and the Sacramental Imagination* (New York: Continuum, 1997). See especially ch. 6, 89-107.

3. Mike Graves, *The Sermon as Symphony: Preaching the Literary Forms of the New Testament* (Valley Forge: Judson Press, 1997).

4. Jana Childers, *Performing the Word: Preaching as Theatre* (Nashville: Abingdon Press, 1998) and Alec Gilmore, *Preaching as Theatre* (London: SCM Press, 1996).

"Hello, how are you?" She responds: "Fine, thank you, and you?" and goes on her way to her office. In that simple transaction both of us acknowledge the essential value of human interaction by obeying socially prescribed rituals of greeting. We are recognizing the presence of one another as partners in a brief encounter. No one describes that transaction as artistic. It does, however, have the potential for becoming art. Were I to take this transaction and script it into a play or a movie, it would be an example of *mimesis*, an occasion where art imitates everyday life.

Similarly, preaching draws upon a rich interplay of transactions not only from worlds of art, but also from everyday life. Think of the different kinds of communications necessary for preaching! The variety of conversations one has, with self, others, the text, and God, provides grist for the homiletical imagination. Ruminations begin to take shape as a *form* for a sermon deemed appropriate for bringing into an assembly of worshippers. No sermon is complete, however, until it becomes a word event—until the *form of the sermon is transformed into human speech and gesture.* We can read sermons as devotional literature. But unless it "gets up off the lectern and takes on flesh" it cannot be called preaching.[5]

Performance is a word that conveys the lively, emergent quality of preaching. Performance literally means "form coming through." Applied to the preaching event, performance describes how the *form* of a sermon comes through the body and voice of the preacher. This is a fuller description of the preaching event than to name it as "the transmission of a message." Preaching is like other performances. A piece of music comes through the voice and body of the singer. A playwright's work comes through when staged in a theater. A sermon reaches its destination, its point of completion, when it arrives in the domain of sound and enactment.

For me, performance is a much better term to use to describe the oral event of preaching than the more conventional term *delivery*. *Delivery* is a perfectly good word, but a tired word, I think, worn out by appearance on innumerable sermon evaluation forms. The word is reminiscent of a time when linear-transmission models of persuasion dominated our thinking about preaching. According to this model, persuasive communication takes place along the straight and narrow line proceeding from the mouth of the preacher to the ear of the listener. What obstructs the flow of the message along that singular trajectory is imaged as noise or interference. The preacher's task is to overcome the obstacles to a clear hearing of the message through proper organization of the message and effective use of the voice. What the preacher hopes to do is to persuade the passive listener that the message is true and applicable to the listener's life. The

---

5. Childers, 20, 26.

preacher's voice and body are the means by which the content of the message is "delivered" to the listener's ear.

This linear model, however, and the word *delivery* seem to flatten the elliptical shape and communal nature of the preaching process. Preaching depends upon a lively interaction between the preacher, God, the text, and the congregation. The roles of speakers, messages, and listeners are constantly reassigned during the composition and performance of a sermon. Sometimes it is God who speaks through a text or through a personal experience, and then who listens as we craft our response. Sometimes the text is given a voice by means of an oral reading, then falls silent as we speak *about* it. Congregations listen but certainly speak by means of body language and even uttered responses in the preaching event. What preacher does not listen to the congregation—their needs, their imagined questions, and concerns—when fashioning a word that is appropriate for the occasion? The relationship between speakers, messages, and listeners is so dynamic and complex that it cannot be accounted for as a straight and narrow line.

Delivery has other unfortunate associations. I think of the one who shows up at my door in a brown uniform. The truck is running. The person delivers a package, not knowing what is in it, having had nothing to do with putting the package together. The task is simply to get me the package, get my signature on a clipboard, get back in the truck, and go.

The one doing the delivering is detached from what is delivered. This hardly seems to fit what we do in speaking an effective sermon. We do know what detachment sounds like when we hear it in the sermon, however. Have you ever listened to a sermon where you sensed a chasm between *what* had been prepared and *how* it was actually spoken? I remember a preacher talking about "the peace that passes all understanding" with such fearful agitation that his wristwatch flew off his arm and went sailing into the congregation! There is often a distance between *what* is being said, and *how*. We hear it in the voice, see it in the body: words of comfort, spoken in a harsh, grating tone; calls to prayer issued in sing-song tonality, obscuring the sense. How do we address this problem of detachment? What words or concepts should we use? What practices can help us overcome the distance between ourselves in the preaching event and the sermon itself?

Performance is useful for addressing the issue of detachment in preaching. Congruity between *what* a preacher says and *how* it is spoken is an element of evocative, effective preaching. John Dominic Crossan nicely elucidates the theological principle undergirding this value in his overture to *The Historical Jesus*: "In the beginning was the performance; not the word alone, not the deed alone, but both, each indelibly marked with the other forever."[6] A performance-centered model of preaching highlights the ways that *what* is said and *how* it is spoken mark one another *indelibly* in the preaching event. Word (the structure of thought) is inextricably bound to deed (the manner of speaking) in the experience of the sermon in performance. This makes for an *authentic* preaching moment.

This constitutive view of performance displaces the proliferation of its pejorative associations in talk about preaching. *Performance* for many preachers is a dirty word. It is often use to describe pretentious, artificial behaviors. Performance is associated with theatricality in everyday life. To say "He is overly *dramatic*!" is a way of describing (and criticizing) a set of vocal and physical mannerisms that call attention to the behavior of the preacher and overwhelm the thought and sense of the sermon. It is well to note that stylistic devices are culturally negotiated. What appears to be dramatic in one church's service of worship might be deemed quite appropriate in another. Determining what is dramatic and what is not has as much to do with the one doing the assessing as it does with the one who is speaking.

A performance-centered model of communication for preaching, however, assumes that all forms of human communication are essentially dramatic. What happens in communication is encounter. Meaning takes on shape and dimension as a speaker says a particular thing in a particular manner for a particular reason. The transaction takes place during a particular time and place for a particular audience! The word *dramatic* has a primary role to play in our talk about human communication; it need not appear as an annoying bit player that calls attention to stylistic excess![7] Human beings make sense of their experience by means of an infinite array of speech acts; whether they shout a word of protest in a rally, speak lovingly to a spouse or partner, or craft a sermon for pulpit performance, human beings are caught within an intricate network of performance practices that define who they are and the values of the communities they inhabit. Performance studies provides a framework for understanding the constitutive aspects of human interaction—it is *making* not *faking*. A performance-centered view of preaching presses the craft of preaching into the sphere of aesthetic communication and understands preaching as a form of enactment and embodied speech. From this angle of vision we can define the sermon as a form of creative

---

6. John Dominic Crossan, *The Historical Jesus: The Life of a Mediterranean Jewish Peasant* (New York: HarperCollins, 1991), xi.

7. For more on this point, see Richard Ward, *Speaking of the Holy: The Art of Communication in Preaching* (St. Louis: Chalice Press, 2001), 25-29.

thought forged from the interrelationship between text and tradition, preacher and congregation; it is a mode of sacred address that is completed in the act of speaking within the context of liturgy.

Performing the Words of Scripture: An Oral Hermeneutic for Preaching

The question is often raised: "Why is Scripture read so poorly in worship? Is there anything that can be done about it?" It is a complicated issue not easily answered. Here I can only offer a clue. I was recently rereading a collection of *Three Church Dramas* by Olov Hartman. In his directions for performances of the pieces, he says "inasmuch as these dramas are marked by a definite *anti-expressionistic* character [italics mine], little movement, gesture or inflection should be employed."[8] The anti-expressionistic style is what has governed most readings of Scripture I have heard. Readers aim for a kind of plain speech that diminishes inflection and tonality in favor of directness and clarity. Unfortunately such readings do not match the liveliness of thought and the play of language offered by the text; when uninflected, they sound flat, and dimensions of meaning are lost.

Liturgical readings of Scripture that are flat and unengaging make the task of preaching from those texts more difficult. If little is communicated to a listener through a public reading of Scripture, why should a listener invest much interest in the text selected for the sermon? The way a text is spoken in the performance of the liturgy says much about the value of that biblical text for that community, and for the sermon that interprets it.

If we invest time and attention in the public reading of Scripture, we will reap benefits in our ministry of proclamation. Training the voice and body to become more responsive to the language, thought, attitudes, and intentions we find in biblical texts will certainly improve the way they are received in worship. *Cultivating these competencies and practices trains us to respond more fully to the expressions, interpretations, and perceptions we present in our own sermons!* The disciplines of oral reading awaken our homiletical imaginations; we gain new hearings of texts that have become overly familiar to us and become interested in texts we do not hear very often. Start reading a text aloud as a part of your preparation to preach and watch how you enter the world of that text more fully! See whether the kind of questions you ask of the text change in some way! In Mark 7:24-30, Jesus encounters a Syro-Phoenician woman. When he responds to her request—"Let the children be fed first! It is not right to take the children's bread and throw it to dogs"—how does he *sound?*

---

8. Trans. by Brita Stendahl (Philadelphia: Fortress Press, 1966), xiv.

What is his state of mind? What is his attitude about the woman? How can that interpretation inform the way you read that exchange aloud?

Eugene Lowry recommends that we look for what is weird in a text, then let it do its work on us.[9] I have found that reading a Scripture aloud, several times, over and over again, focusing on different characters each time, opens up the weirdness of a text in startling ways. I recommend that preachers return frequently to a sermon text at different points during their preparation process and reread it aloud. Soon it becomes so familiar that they can read it *as if the words they are reading are their own.* That is a goal for both lectors or preachers: *What do I have to know about this text if I am going to read it as if the words are my own?* Working with that question makes for better public reading in worship, and for better exegesis in preaching.

Performance theory teaches that the voice and body are not simply instruments for reading a text aloud; they are a means of exploring the world of that text. Giving voice to Scripture means transforming words fixed in print into an experience of sound and sense. Sometimes specific movements are suggested by the actions characters in a biblical narrative perform: "bowing down," or "running out to meet" someone. Or we hear of how Jesus looks upon a character and loves him. Some of these actions can be fully embodied in the performance of a text; others can only be suggested. When we pay attention to these explicit actions of characters in the text, we are paying attention to its *kinesthetic* elements and adding dimension to our experience of it. Our voices and bodies will give us clues as to how words and phrases might be spoken, even when explicit actions are not given. When we look for ways to speak the text as if the words were our own, we must pay attention to the rhythm and pace of language as it flows from the page through us to the listener. We will look for words to emphasize, places to pause for emphasis. Soon the distance between what is on the page and what is being uttered is closed. Both performer and audience are caught up in the immediate address of the words in that text. When we share in that experience of being addressed by words of Scripture, it is as if the author is present in the assembly, even if the identity of that author is disputed. A text in performance is not simply a communicative event, but a way of being present to that text.

Students and scholars of the Bible have long noted the proximity of the written tradition to oral form. Texts bear the residue of the oral traditions they arose from and prompt oral responses in the form of sermons,

---

9. Eugene Lowry, "Surviving the Sermon Preparation Process," *Journal for Preachers* 32:3 (Easter 2001): 29.

songs, and litanies. Taking oral form seriously as a hermeneutical strategy, we discover what the discipline of performance studies has long noted—that performance not only deepens our appreciation of the *aesthetic* values of biblical texts, it helps us *know* and *understand* these texts at a deeper level. What better place to preach from than the vantage point of performance?

Joanne Buchanan Brown developed the following sermon in a course I taught where methods and concepts described in this article were employed. We began with a communal exegesis of John 21:1-19. Part of our process included hearing the entire narrative recited. This was an important feature of our preliminary work because we rarely have the chance to hear a long biblical narrative performed. When it is, we are better able to hear how pericopes are woven into a larger literary fabric! Questions about the interrelationships of literary units within the whole narrative arise more quickly and easily than when the narrative is read in silence. To broaden the horizons of the text is to expand the opportunity for finding connections and juxtapositions between the lived experience of the text and the living experiences of our own "storied" existence.

Our process in class was to find such points of connection and dissonance between the text from John's gospel and our own experiences lived before God. We found that an approach based in an *oral and communal* hermeneutic yielded intriguing homiletical insight. Jesus' words, "Come, have breakfast!" prompted a memory for Joanne that she enacted in the sermon. Read the sermon out loud and listen for the word of God!

It's early morning, just after dawn. The sun is a ball of orange on the horizon. The man stands on the seashore alone and watches. Finally, he can be silent no longer, and calls to the weary fishermen who have been at it all night.

"Not catching any, huh? Move to the other side, the right side—yeah, over there. You'll get some there."

And, indeed as soon as the net is cast on the right, the fish come out of nowhere and the net is full in no time. Now the problem is that it's too heavy to haul in!

There is a gleeful shout from the boat: "It's the Lord!" And the fisherman named Peter can't wait to get to him. Suddenly his energy is bursting, like the net. He quickly belts his outer clothes, mumbling something like, "Hot diggity dog, Jesus is back! I can't wait for these guys to get it together—I'm gone! I'm coming, Lord." And Peter jumps into the sea, as Peter tends to do.

Well, when everyone gets to shore there is a crackling little fire of hospitality going, and the smell of grilling fish and toast is thick in the salty air. "Bring some of the fresh catch," says the host on the beach. "It's time for breakfast!"

The fishermen, tired, achy, and pretty grimy after their night of disappointment at work, are grateful for a hot breakfast served to them by their teacher and friend. "Great fish, Master! Done to perfection. Even the bread tastes different over a campfire."

With the sun climbing higher, the seagulls circling and calling in their game of tag at the water's edge, their Lord is here with them, alive again. Life is good. Silently the men bask in this moment together.

I remember those long midnights in charge of the Emergency Room twenty years ago. The "graveyard shift," some folks called it. Especially if there was a full moon—that was the worst! Babies being born all over the place before we could even get the mothers upstairs to deliver. Combative drivers "under the influence" being dropped off by the police. Kids who had swallowed toys or played with firecrackers in the middle of the night. Domestic violence victims shaking and crying, afraid to be there, afraid not to be. Traumas, accidents, and heart attacks 'til there wasn't a monitor bed left.

And some nights, nobody was saved. Some nights it was a weary, grimy, gruesome business. But then, oh, around 7:30 or so in the morning, the call might come, "Joanne, pick up line 2, please, Joanne, line 2."

(Please, God, not another trauma call. It's almost time to go!) "This is Joanne." "Hi, honey, it's Mom. Want to come by for breakfast on your way home?" Suddenly, I'd perk up. "Yeah. I'd love to, Mom. I never got a break last night and I'm starving. Thanks! I'm hoping to get out of here on time. I'll see you around 8:45. Bye."

"Boy, you sure came back to life! Who was that?" one of the docs would tease. But I would just smile myself through the next hour and get to my mother's tiny dinette in the maroon house on Normandy Road, where coffee, orange juice, that thick, chubby French bread toast, and the aroma of the hickory smoked bacon and frying eggs all awaited me. We

would greet each other with a hug and kiss and she'd say "Go ahead and sit down, honey. Everything's ready." My mother, a cheerful early-riser, would have already eaten. But she'd serve me and sit with me while I, numbed by the night, replenished myself on her cooking, and her presence.

And then, after breakfast, we would talk. She would ask me questions about my life, and my loves, and the general state of my soul. She would ask: "How's work?" and "How did your date go last Friday?" and "When are you going to get off midnights, honey?" and "Do you need some money for that car repair?" Sometimes the questions would get harder: "Did you take care of those kids who died in the car accident last week?" and "Do you think you'll ever get married again?" and "Have you thought any more about missionary work lately?" and "Are you happy, sweetie?"

It has occurred to me recently that my mother, though she was asking me things, was really telling me things. She was telling me, "I care about who you are." "You are precious to me." "I want you to be a responsible person for God." In those breakfast mornings together, my mother, my best friend and teacher, through her cooking, her hospitality, and her questions was really telling me, in every way she could, "I love you."

Breakfast is over now for Jesus and Peter, too, here on the lakeshore. Fish bones are being scraped off plates and the last of the toast has been offered around. And now the after-breakfast talk begins. Everyone knows it's coming. For as much as Jesus likes to dine with company, his friends remember it is not the food, but the conversation, the instruction, the proclamation that happens around the meal that has always been the main event.

"Simon, son of John, do you love me?" (Now, this is serious; this is like my mother calling me "Joanne Faye.")

I wonder what Peter thinks about this formality? Jesus uses the name Peter had before he was renamed as one of the twelve. Does Peter think, "Oh, oh, here it comes. He's disowning me, and I deserve it"? Or is he just relieved that Jesus is asking him about his love at all? At any rate, he answers, "Yes, Lord, You know that I love you." (Well, that wasn't too painful . . .)

But two seconds later, "Simon, son of John, do you love me?" (What, has he lost his hearing since the Resurrection? Better say it louder.) "Yes, Lord, you know that I love you."

And now a third time, "Simon, son of John, do you love me?" (For cry-ing out loud, Lord, now this hurts. This really does. Why do you keep asking me if you don't believe me?) "Lord, you know everything; you know that I love you."

And Peter is right. Jesus knows. Everything. He knows that Peter is still Peter, no matter by what name he calls him. The same Peter who said, with his knees shaking and his heart sinking, "I do not know the man." And denied Jesus three times.

Does Jesus ask Peter if Peter loves him three times to charge Peter for his three denials? Could be, but I have another idea. I think Jesus isn't asking Peter anything. I think maybe he is telling Peter three times "I love you" to cancel out Peter's three denials. In fact, if Peter "got it," he might have sung, "Yes, Jesus loves me. Yes, Jesus loves me. Yes, Jesus loves me. Because he told me so."

The last meal my mother cooked for me was not breakfast, but a big pot of her famous beef stew. You see, she was dying, but she came home from the hospital to cook and serve that stew. It was unfinished business she came back to finish. She wanted to tell me that she loved me one last time, over a meal. So we sat, and we ate, and after the meal, we talked, and she asked me questions—and then she entrusted to me the sacred recipe for her special beef stew.

Is this unfinished business for Jesus—this feeding his sheep one more time? This trying to tell Peter something with his questions? Knowing how human Peter is, Jesus can't really trust Peter's words of commitment, can he? And yet Peter can trust his Lord's. Could it be that Jesus can tell Peter, "Feed my sheep" (care for my people, lead my Church), that he can entrust to Peter the work to be carried on not necessarily because Peter loves Jesus, but because Jesus loves Peter?

Perhaps "Simon, son of John, do you love me?" becomes "I care about who you are." "You are precious to me." "I want you to be a responsi-ble person for God." "I trust you with my sheep." "I love you."

The next time Jesus calls you for breakfast, or in front of his crack-ling fire, or around his table, give your best attention to the conversa-tion. Will there be unfinished business? An entrusting of some kind? Questions? Maybe, but perhaps, just perhaps, the risen Christ will just be trying to tell you how much you are loved—and, because of that, you are entrusted.

Richard Ward is Associate Professor of Preaching and Performance Studies at the Iliff School of Theology, Denver, Colorado.

Joanne Buchanan-Brown is Pastor of Lyons United Methodist Church, Lyons, Colorado.

9

PREACHING TOWARD COLLEGIAL EXCELLENCE

EVE OF PENTECOST—EVENSONG

Stay Close, Please!

1 Peter 2:4-10
Mitties McDonald DeChamplain

GREETINGS! It is lovely to see the "elect" from every Episcopal seminary gathered here this evening to begin the first Preaching Excellence Program of the twenty-first century! This will be a week of glorious intensity. We will pray, preach, make Eucharist, listen, and gather homiletical insights day and night for the next five days. This is not an event for the fainthearted! But we are blessed, I think, to begin our work together on the Eve of Pentecost. Tonight is an ideal occasion to remember that God the Holy Spirit—the giver and the Lord of life—puts breath in us to enliven our preaching. And so, in rough paraphrase of the salutation in 1 Peter: May grace and peace and inspiration be yours in abundance throughout the coming week.

We will travel tomorrow to celebrate the Feast of Pentecost at the National Cathedral, a place described as a "sermon carved in stone." There, I had an epiphany I would like to share with you as we begin our time together.

In February 1995, after a gathering of homiletics professors at the College of Preachers, I made my first visit to the cathedral. I was dispirited and weary, having recently completed General Ordination Exams. Colleagues urged me, as a remedy for post-GOE blues, to attend the cathedral's principal Sunday service at eleven o'clock.

The liturgical precision and majesty of the worship were wonderful to behold. I stepped forward to receive communion. The usher guiding me into place was an elegant woman in her mid-sixties with radiant ebony skin. Her eyes brimmed with an almost incandescent warmth. In a kind and gentle voice, she said to each of us who came forward: "Stay close, please. Stay close, please. Stay close, please." With those words she nudged

123

us elbow to elbow around the railing—far closer together than I would typically be to strangers. The words were surely offered to expedite the administering of communion, but, in an instant, the sinking, stone-cold feeling I had carried with me into church was gone. I felt secure, grounded, alive again.

I reckon that the words "Stay close, please" are about as theologically significant as three words can be. Not a bad motto for Christian living: "Stay close, please." Stay close to God and to each other—rightly related, connected. That moment of connection and solidarity in the cathedral comes to mind in relation to the words from 1 Peter: "Come to him, a living stone, though rejected by mortals yet chosen and precious in God's sight, and like living stones, let yourselves be built into a spiritual house, to be a holy priesthood, to offer spiritual sacrifices acceptable to God through Jesus Christ."

In a sense, the usher in the cathedral was helping the congregation to be built into a spiritual house. Even if she was not aware of it, she preached a powerful sermon. "Stay close, please" is a distillation of the good news that the Christian life is meant to be lived in community, in Christ. The preaching life, as we all know well, also happens in community. We come this week like living stones, to feed each other with the word of God in our sermons, to feed on Christ in the prayers and the breaking of bread, and to be built into something new. We may have to preach our sermons by ourselves, but we never preach alone. We are called into being as preachers through the agency of other persons. There is no "me" as a preacher without "us." We find our own true preaching voices in relationship—through communion and in communication with the other.

A natural expectation of preachers is that the more we preach, the more self-confident we will become, and the more self-confident we become, the better our preaching will be: "Practice makes perfect." But self-confidence *per se* may actually be death to preaching excellence, if the desire for self-confidence distracts us from the practice of acknowledging our dependence on God. Maybe the more we preach, the less self-confident we ought to become! Christ our confidence alone! We have grounds for hope and joy in our preaching because the ground on which we stand, from which we preach, is Jesus Christ, the living stone. Christ is the Word that gives us speech. By virtue of this, we preach with abandon, with total self-forgetfulness and authentic self-offering. We can "go for broke" in our preaching because of the One who broke himself open for us in love, a perfect sacrifice and self-offering for the whole world.

One of our tasks this week is to remember anew that the work of the Incarnation goes forward, by the mercies of God, in and through ordinary people like you and me. For we are "a chosen race, a royal priesthood, a holy nation, God's own people, in order that [we] may proclaim the mighty acts of him who called [us] out of darkness into his marvelous light." And we are not chosen for this work of proclamation because we are worthy, we are worthy because we are chosen, made precious and able by the one who holds us all fast within the reach of his saving embrace. We place ourselves in Love's way this week, seeking and serving Christ in one another as we preach, confident that the Holy Spirit will teach us what we know not, give us what we have not, and make us what we are not, for Christ's sake. And so, dear preachers of God: Stay close, please. Stay close, please. Stay close, please.

Mitties McDonald DeChamplain is Trinity Church Professor of Preaching at The General Theological Seminary in New York City.

VOTIVE OF THE HOLY SPIRIT

Of Snakes, Scorpions, and the Holy Spirit

1 Corinthians 12:4-11; Luke 11:9-13
Joe G. Burnett

THERE WE WERE at graveside on a bleak, overcast day: Grandparents on both sides of the family, parents, a brother and sister. Surrounding and enfolding these sad, cold faces were dozens of parishioners who knew and loved one or more of them. The words offered up as we neared the end of the committal service seemed impotent in the wake of this daughter's suicide: "Grant, O Lord, to all who are bereaved the spirit of faith and courage, that they may have strength to meet the days to come with steadfastness and patience; not sorrowing as those without hope, but in thankful remembrance of your great goodness . . . "

These mournful kin were weary from years of failed attempts to help Carol beat her depression. They were overcome with fresh memories of her frail body, found drugged to death on her apartment floor. Today was too early for this prayerful cry to the Holy Spirit to make much difference. But, in time, it would. Before long they would receive and appropriate God's healing balm, going on with life and faith. The parish, there for them in their nighttime of loss, would be with them when joy returned in the morning. The liturgy that had sustained them in good times past would come alive for them again.

As we left the grave and returned to our cars, another emotionally laden time of prayer was taking place almost a thousand miles away, where many others also felt themselves on the threshold of life and death. It was a General Convention of Episcopalians keeping silence, invoking the Spirit, waiting—waiting to see how yet another attempt to transcend sexual barriers would fare, how yet another attempt to alter time-honored liturgical language would end up. Those who hoped to hold the line, and those who hoped to march into a new day—all praying for the gift of the Spirit. What year this was? A reasonable hunch might be last summer. Reasonable—but wrong. These events took place in 1976, in Jackson, Mississippi, and Minneapolis, Minnesota, where the General Convention gave us the first reading of a new Prayer Book, and unprecedented approval of the ordination of women.

I recount this curious juxtaposition of events because it illustrates the intertwining of two common threads in our community of faith: the day-to-day pastoral realities of ordinary congregational life—the love and loss, joy and sorrow, comings and goings, that mark our passages over generations—and the ongoing conflict over policies of the Church as a whole. I recently visited with a bishop who had been reading Jan Karon's popular "Mitford" books about the life and times of Father Tim, tireless vicar of the pristine little Episcopal church in Appalachian Americana. The bishop was not impressed. He shared his frustration with the complexity of ministry in the twenty-first century, concluding with a grin, "Toto, we're not in Mitford any more!"

In one sense he's right—we've *never* been in Mitford. It is twenty-five years since Minneapolis. In 2003, again in Minneapolis, we will see a Church still struggling over issues of liturgy and sexuality—over how best to present the gospel in a postmodern society.

Yet in another sense, we're *always* in Mitford. For during these same years, parishes and missions of all sorts and sizes have experienced the ceaseless round of birth and death, the ordinary cycles of daily life that draw people together in bonds of love and care, and the mundane struggles, quarrels, and hypocrisies that annoy and maybe mature us.

These two worlds, Mitford and Minneapolis, inevitably collide. This is why I am perplexed when I hear some folks talk about their grand diocesan schemes for evangelism and church growth. They boast of new church starts and outreach to seekers, all of which, they say, will bypass the needless conflicts of the "national church." That placeless, faceless designation seems to describe a gathering that exists only to air unnecessary grievances and fight over issues ordinary folks don't care about.

Recently I did a mental review of every congregation with which I have worked closely during twenty-seven years of ordained ministry. I couldn't think of a single one untouched in some significant way by the controversial social issues these evangelists intend to ignore. In *Amazing Grace*, Kathleen Norris describes a congregation in South Dakota scandalized to learn that a beloved older couple, members for years, had been living out of wedlock all that time. She then tells of another congregation where a long-time deacon proudly defended the parish's decision to invite the organist, a known homosexual, to join the church board. "He's one of us," said the man. "We know we can trust him."

Whether in Mitford or Minneapolis, the Church today finds such issues woven into the fabric of its being. They wear the faces of people who sit in the pews and go to the rail right next to us. Some of them are "we." This is the reality of the Church wherein we live and serve. To do evangelism, the first requirement is to be honest about who we are.

How do those of us charged with responsibility for pastoral leadership, priestly ministry, and preaching stay faithful to this task in the midst of such conflict and diversity? I think the lessons for today's votive Eucharist "Of the Holy Spirit" yield unexpected, even stunning insights. This passage in Luke is set in the context of Jesus' teaching on prayer. The disciples plead, "Lord, teach us to pray." Jesus offers them a model for prayer embodying the whole of human concern. Then he emphasizes the need for persistence. "Ask, and it will be given you; search, and you will find; knock, and the door will be opened for you. If your child asks for a fish, will you give a snake? Or for an egg, will you give a scorpion? How much more then will the heavenly Father give the Holy Spirit to those who ask?"

All true prayer invokes the Spirit, whether for a grieving family at graveside, or for a conflicted Church in convention. But there is more to this than meets the eye. To understand this "gift of the Holy Spirit to those who ask" we must see how Luke envisions this promise ultimately fulfilled. Luke believes that the return of Jesus may be postponed indefinitely. Thus his story, as one scholar puts it, makes "room for the Church in history." Essential to this continuing ministry of witness and presence is remembering and re-appropriating the gospel in the unfolding situations of everyday life—when Jesus himself is no longer physically present with his disciples.

Throughout Luke's narrative we have glimpses of this paradox: absence and impending presence. When Jesus gathers with the disciples for the upper room meal he astonishes them with this announcement: "I will not eat or drink of this Passover until the kingdom of God comes."

When the two on the road to Emmaus invite the stranger they bring with them to table, suddenly he is revealed to be the risen Lord. Then just as suddenly he is gone again, vanished from their sight. In the closing verses of the Gospel—and the opening verses of Acts—we are confronted with what seems to be his ultimate withdrawal in the Ascension. But in and through the gift of the Spirit even this most dramatic absence is transformed into an enduring, accessible, universal presence. The missionary church that heeds its Lord's urging—to ask, and search, and knock—does so believing that the God who raised Jesus from the dead will not respond to these requests with empty promises—with "snakes and scorpions"—but with the living presence of the risen Christ, in and through the power of the Spirit.

This has radical implications for life, ministry, and preaching in the Church. These implications become still more profound when we come to terms with Paul's earlier articulation of the Church as the body of Christ. He regarded this as the language of a dawning new age. And, of course, it still is, but in ways he never dreamed. "Now you are the body of Christ," he says to the Corinthian Christians, "and individually members of it." Addressing a deeply conflicted Corinthian community, Paul tells them that their very differences, their individuality, their separateness, are part and parcel of a more fundamental organic unity. Then, he says, their unity, in diversity—their body—is Christ himself. And they, severally, individually, are members of it. They—we—are members of Christ.

Indeed, the Church becomes, in words Anglican tradition has long embraced, the very extension of the Incarnation. In this continuing community, the Risen Christ is discerned and known: First, in the Eucharistic bread that is both sign and symbol of his sacramental body. Second, in the charisms for ministry that embody and sustain his sacrificial service. Finally, in freedom and wisdom for ordering the body's common life.

Now here's the rub for those of us who preach: in 1976 as I stood with that family whose daughter had taken her own life, the gifts of the spirit for ministry were being exercised in and by a community whose ancient texts were silent about the ethics of suicide. And the gathering in Minneapolis that voted in a new prayer book and approved the ordination of women was doing so without explicit instructions from Luke or Paul or anyone else in the scriptural canon. The deeds and decisions of both communities that day were guided and guarded by a higher power: the tangible, corporeal presence of Christ, in the form of the body of which they were the members, in and through the power of the Spirit.

It is ironic now to think that Paul, himself once a persecutor of the Church on scriptural grounds, was the one who helped that very Church claim the freedom to think beyond the inherent limitations of its scriptural heritage. He made it possible for someone like Luke, a Gentile, to be admitted to the community of the new covenant. And neither Paul nor Luke could have foreseen the multitude of ways that the fledgling Church would face similar unprecedented questions in its unfolding life. They could not and did not speak specifically on the changing roles of women, medical abortion, the technologies of prolonging or ending life, the AIDS epidemic, or same-sex partnerships, just to name a few.

Yet the Church, as they envisioned it—living in the paradox of the absence and yet greater presence of the risen Jesus—would be a Church set free to contend with new occasions, new duties, and new divisions. A Church gifted with wisdom, knowledge, and faith, empowered to think, speak, act and minister—and even do evangelism—in the midst of these realities, however unpleasant, whether in Jerusalem or Rome, Mitford or Minneapolis. Their grasp of the gospel of God would light the Church's way to the dawning of each new age in ways they never dreamed.

Wisdom, knowledge, faith—and courage: these gifts are yet manifest among us. For we are the body of Christ, and individually members of it. These gifts help us to preach, as simply and as urgently as Jesus taught us to pray: to ask what the Spirit is saying to the churches; to search out the presence of Christ in unexpected ways and places; and to knock on the doors of seemingly intractable dilemmas and unanswerable questions. Today's generations of inquiring minds and hungry hearts need the good news of God's generosity, and they confront us with an urgent prayer. May we who preach be prepared to give them more than scorpions and snakes.

Joe G. Burnett is Professor of Pastoral Theology at The School of Theology, University of the South, Sewanee, Tennessee.

EVENSONG

When the Student Is Ready, the Teacher Appears

Psalm 44; 2 Corinthians 5:11–6:2; Luke 17:1-10
Lisa Kraske Cressman

MY DAD was appalled. He grilled me with his questions and his eyes. "The parish actually shouted the bishop down?"

Inwardly, I groaned. Up to that point it had been such a pleasant trip! I had been relating a story to my parents. We were enjoying dinner on a gorgeous spring evening. I was recounting that one of the congregations in my diocese had invited the bishop to have a conversation about an issue in the national church about which they were upset. But instead of a genuine dialogue, members of the gathered assembly shouted the bishop down to the point that further conversation was suspended.

"How is that possible in the Church?" my dad demanded, with rising anger. "How can members of the Church behave just like people in society do? People in society are getting more and more selfish, their behavior more appalling. How can the Church act just like society? If the Church can't teach appropriate behavior, what hope is there for the world?"

I was on risky ground. My dad has had a chip on his shoulder about the Church for twenty-five years, a chip roughly the size of a redwood tree. He had been a member of the vestry when a perceived hypocrisy drove him from the Church, an episode he's never been willing to discuss. The only time he's been to church since is for his children's weddings, my ordinations, some funerals, and musical concerts. I knew I wasn't only answering his immediate question. The Church at large was on trial, and I was principle witness for the defense.

I can't often claim that God and I have much in common. But I took comfort in that tense moment, knowing that God has frequently been put on trial as well. The psalmists often demanded that God answer to them for alleged acts of commission and omission.

In Psalm 44 God's supposedly chosen and favorite people have probably just lost a major war and been taken as slaves. The psalmist says that the people remember the stories of God's great deeds for them way back when. God formed them as a people, gave them some terrific land to call their own, helped them win lots of battles, and seemed to take particular pleasure in them. They knew they were special, unique in all creation.

But then, the psalmist cries, you rejected us! You threw us out of our land, trampled us underfoot, scattered us to the four winds. We thought you would win a battle again for us as you've done before. But not only did we lose, we were defeated so badly we've become a derogatory cliche among other nations. We're the original "losers," a laughingstock for the world!

Facing my dad and wondering how to address his rancor, I felt, paradoxically, both like God, who has often been put on trial, and like Israel, who had become laughingstocks and "losers" (which, my dad was saying, is what the Church has become). The obvious hypocrisy of our members' behavior with the bishop had debased the Church and confirmed the other hypocrisies my father had experienced. Not only was I now a witness for the Church's defense, I was also accused of partial responsibility for her demise. As one of the clergy, my dad was saying, I had not seen to the proper raising of God's children. To my dad, the only foundation remaining upon which the Church still stood was paper-thin integrity—and that was cracking.

By God's grace, however, I did not feel ice cracking under my feet. I felt firmly established rock. Jesus told his disciples that bad behavior in the Church is inevitable. There will always be those who cause members to stumble. But, Jesus says, make sure you're not a source of stumbling. Keep the Good News foremost on your minds. Don't be distracted by the egocentrism of society. Don't limit forgiveness: it can't be quantified. Forgive all the members of the Church, no matter how many times they behave badly and shout the bishop down. Nurture both the likable and the unlikable with love and compassion, respect and mercy, accountability and boundaries. Nurture them as a servant nurtures an owner's farms and fields. And when the owner returns, remember your places as servants who did not create the farm, but are only asked to tend it.

The expanse of bedrock under my feet didn't end with Jesus' words. Paul added acreage. Remember the work of reconciliation, he tells the Corinthians. Be a bridge, uniting estranged people to one another and to God. Remember: we don't do this work for ourselves, but for him who died and rose for us. Remember that, even in the midst of strife and discord, salvation is still our present reality and future hope. We need always to be in our right minds—responsive to the claims of divine love and to the needs of people.

So at the dinner table with my dad, I sat, undergirded with God who has been both witness and accused, with Israel the derided, with Jesus and Paul. I also felt acutely what was at stake for one member of the Church's disenfranchised who sat with me at table. I took a deep breath. "Well, Dad, the Church is made up of members of society. People bring into church what they're taught from all sorts of places. The Church strives to add another influence, but it can't control what people do or how they behave. It seems to me that our society is in its adolescence. We're living in an unprecedented age of wealth, leisure, education, power, and individualism. While those are tremendous gifts, we haven't learned what to do with that much freedom. We're like a teenager who's just gotten her driver's license and she's ready to go cruising. She's intoxicated by the power, control, and freedom of the car, but she hasn't developed emotionally to the point of driving with care, purpose, and gratitude.

"I think that society is going to get a lot worse before it gets better. We're going to go down the tubes even further until people wake up and realize the way we're living—unacceptable to one another, to the planet, and to God. The Church's job is to be ready to share the Gospel with them.

"There's a saying of an Eastern religious tradition that sums up one purpose of the Church: 'When the student is ready the teacher appears.' When our society is ready to learn to live with care, purpose, and gratitude for the wealth that we have in all of its forms, the Church can be ready to introduce them to our Teacher, Jesus Christ, and share with them his Good News. In spite of the negative influences society has, I feel boundless hope. We can be ready to teach reconciliation, love, respect, and mercy as soon as the students appear. When the students are ready, so do we need to be."

There was silence at the end of my monologue. I sat anxiously, my fork suspended in my hand. I had as much admitted that the Church doesn't have the kind of societal control my dad demands. I wondered if I had just driven my father even further from the Church.

Then I saw understanding spread across his face. He was ready to hear me. He was ready to acknowledge the me-first culture that has encroached upon many in the Church. He was ready to have confirmed his own belief that our society is probably going to implode on itself before it's willing to be resurrected. And he was willing to hope that the Church is still a major player in the unfolding drama of the Good News on earth.

I doubt my dad's openness is typical. And he was not converted to the point that he'll be returning to the Church, but at least I'm pretty sure he'll show up for my future child's baptism! Yet he does give me hope for a society that has largely forgotten the Church, shoved it aside, mocked and vilified it. To society, the Church is a "loser."

Some of that reaction may be deserved because of how our members treat one another. So if we as leaders of the Church are to have an authentic voice then we must first be students, willing to learn from our Teacher, Jesus Christ. To keep his Good News, to tend it, and not to get distracted either by the bad behavior of our members, or by our detractors, is to remain on bedrock. To observe and critique our society, to pray and study, to love and reconcile, to serve not ourselves but him who died and rose for us, is how we preach salvation as Paul did—salvation now and yet unfolding.

We don't need to be witnesses for the defense, nor take on the expectations of others. We need only to be students of Christ, ready to learn ourselves, as simple and as difficult as that is. If we can do that, then when the students are ready, so will we be. Ready to lead them to the Teacher.

Lisa Kraske Cressman is Rector of St. Thomas' Church,
Whiteland, Indiana.

EMBER DAY

See How the Fields Are Ripe for Harvesting!

John 4:31-42
John W. Conrad

THIS IS AN Ember Day, when we reflect on our callings to ordained ministry. The color in the chapel is purple, the color of penitence—implying that those who presume to hear another's confession ought to be penitents themselves. In keeping with that, let me offer my own confession.

Two months ago I received my preaching assignment for this conference. I read the lessons and filed them away in the back of my brain so I could live with them and let life help me interpret the texts. Shortly thereafter, my mother had a serious stroke. Things were touch and go for a week. In cool, rational discussions over cocktails, my mother had decided to decline all heroic measures and life support. Somehow, in the heat of the moment, it all seemed different. A complication of the stroke was that my mother could not eat. Though alert, communicative, even humorous at times, if she did not recover the ability to swallow, or were not put on a feeding tube, she would slowly starve to death. "How long might that take?" I asked the doctor. "It could take three or four months," he said. I thought: "Do you not say, 'Four more months, then comes the harvest'?"

Prior to her stroke and well into her eighties, my mother was a self-possessed, independent, powerful woman. She had levered herself into an upper-level executive position in a major Los Angeles corporation forty years before Women's Liberation. She was a successful writer and editor.

After the stroke, as they wheeled her out on a gurney she said, "I'm sorry I didn't finish reading the proofs."

My mother did not take well to the constraints imposed on her by her failing body. Used to having Congressmen return her calls personally, she didn't enjoy waiting for the attention of a nurse. She was "Resistant to Care"—a euphemism for angry, loud, demanding, expressing oneself in colorful "nautical" vocabulary. Shortly after I was able to get her into a comfortable nursing home, she got herself thrown out by attempting to commit suicide. She was sent to a different hospital for "psychiatric evaluation." It was a couple of days before I could visit at her new residence. She was asleep when I arrived. Standing at the edge of her bed, feeling useless, I glanced over at the television and saw something vaguely familiar—a helicopter view of Granite Hills High School in El Cajon, California. Terrified, I realized that there was another school shooting in progress. My daughter Julie was a student there. Someone was shooting at my daughter.

There I stood frozen between two loves, two places, two times, and two cultures; between a life all but over and, please God, a life with an abundant future. I heard the words "Do you not say, 'Four more months, then comes the harvest'? But I say to you look around you and see how the fields are ripe for harvesting."

In a moment I realized that for a long time I had been concentrating my energies in one small part of God's creation, ignoring the rest. I had stood and prayed by a lot of bedsides. I had been scrupulous about the pastoral care of my own "flock," but ignored the sheep that had strayed or were never invited into the flock. I had spent time in my own church, own office, and parish hall; but I had done nothing at Granite Hills High School. I had spent a great deal of time tending a crop in a corner, while generally ignoring the wider field in which God has called us to serve. "Do you not say, 'Four more months, then comes the harvest'? But I say to you look around you and see how the fields are ripe for harvesting."

Look around you, and see the fields. One way to look around is on the Internet. Soon after my conversion I logged on to AOL, and clicked on their "Belief Net, "where matters of faith are discussed. The lead article was an interview with a man named Marilyn Manson—who had named himself after a suicidal sex symbol and mass murderer. His bizarre, diabolical ideas on the meaning of life were spread not only across the screen, but available for audio-feed as well. I went to the search engine, and typed in "Episcopal." There were no listings. I typed "Christian" and found many. But the first few articles I read were full of anger, bigotry, exclusion, and self-righteousness—nothing like the Good News I know. The "harvest" on the Internet seems rotting in the field.

Another way to look into the world is through television. I remember an early episode of "The X Files," a program purporting to explore the supernatural. One of the characters is Scully, a woman with an M.D., employed by the FBI to explore events in the X Files. Scully is self-assured and drop-dead gorgeous. She is also a scientific fundamentalist, one who believes everything that happens can be explained in scientific terms—a perfect person to explore inexplicable events that find their way into the X Files. One day, however, she encounters an event she cannot explain, someone who comes back to life, like Lazarus: one minute scientifically dead, the next minute fully alive. Scully's world is hurled into crisis.

Raised a Roman Catholic, she returns to a church and enters a confessional. The young priest asks what she wants to confess. She replies that she does not want to make a confession but to ask a question. "Do you believe in miracles?" she asks. Of course that isn't her real question. What she wants to know is whether there is a God at work in the world. The priest says something inane about every sunrise being a miracle. Scully finds this unsatisfactory. She is grasping for a belief system better than her own. Having failed in his call as an apostle and evangelist, the priest lapses into the default position of unsure clergy—amateur therapist. "How are you feeling?" he asks. "I feel afraid," she says. The faux therapist in collar asks, "What are you afraid of?" After a pause Scully answers, "I'm afraid that God is really talking to us and no one is listening."

People who do polls tell us that about 60 percent of this country's population are not practicing Christians. Scully stands for something like twenty million people in America who are scientific fundamentalists. From time to time, some of these souls, some of this harvest, will encounter God in ways they cannot explain. If we are open and inviting they just may come to us for answers. But they probably won't come to us as Scully did, on their knees. Are we prepared to answer their questions? Do the people of our congregations know how to talk about the work of God in the world? Have we gone into the world and let it know that the Episcopal Church is a place to come when exploring the spiritual path? Have we done anything at all about the fields that are ready for harvesting?

My mother is going to be okay. With God's help she is wrestling with the latest challenges that life has foisted upon her, and she can eat a little now. She receives communion every week from a Lay Eucharistic Minister. The church that she cared for is now caring for her. She is safe and secure. Soon she will be swept into the loving embrace of our Lord Jesus. But my lovely daughter Julie . . . I worry about her. I worry about the world she will have to live in, and I wonder if there aren't some things you and I, by the grace of God, can do about it. "Do you not say, 'Four more months, then comes the harvest'? But I say to you look around you and see how the fields are ripe for harvesting."

John W. Conrad is Rector of St. Albans' Church,
El Cajon, California.

FEAST OF SAINT COLUMBA

Seeing Snakes

Luke 10:17-20
Rhonda Smith McIntire

THIS SERMON began some time ago with a four-foot-long, fat black bull snake on my front porch. He crawled by, and all the atavistic sensations you can imagine kicked right in. I just *knew* a whole den of giant snakes was under the house plotting how to come up through the toilet and eat me while I was sleeping.

Today, we celebrate the Feast of St. Columba, whose appointed Gospel lesson reports Jesus saying to the disciples, "See, I have given you authority to tread on snakes . . . and over all the power of the enemy; and nothing will hurt you." I did not think about that particular passage when the black bull snake slithered by. Instead, I thought of the myths where the serpent is Satan in the Garden of Eden and poisonous vipers are used by God to punish the whiners in the wilderness.

Thank goodness I have a wise friend who challenged me to move past my fear. She reminded me that Moses healed the whining Israelites with a bronze serpent, and that the caduceus with its two snakes is the symbol of medicine. Then, she, herself a Buddhist, said, "And, Rhonda, isn't it true that the shape of the bishop's staff has something to do with Moses' bronze serpent?"

Not long after, a rattlesnake greeted me as I returned from a morning walk. In case you've forgotten, rattlesnakes *are* poisonous. Luckily, it was around Thanksgiving. We were having a cold spell, so even though she shook her rattles at me, she couldn't muster enough stamina to coil and strike. I decided that *one* snake is one thing, but *two* are a *sign.* So, I started looking up things about snakes. You know, they used to be considered holy. Snakes have been symbols not only for healing but also for protection, fertility, cleverness, eternal life. In ancient Akkadian, the word "priest" means "snake charmer."

I'm a priest. I'd seen two snakes. Carl Jung surely would say the synchronicity should not be ignored. Then, John Butcher sent me a copy of his new book. His take on snakes was entirely new to me. He writes, "Look for the recurring symbol of the serpent in Holy Scripture for its meaning. In the Garden of Eden, it is the serpent who has a very necessary function—*to present choices.* In the wilderness, Moses holds up a bronze serpent for the people to see, and they know they have choices to make in their journey through the wilderness. In the teachings of Jesus we are reminded to be 'wise as serpents.'" Butcher goes on, "Whenever a serpent appears in a story, *someone has to make a decision.* [Dealing with] serpents means that when the power of the Resurrected Jesus is alive within us, we become better at handling our decisions."[1]

Today we remember that St. Columba bravely sailed from Ireland to cold Iona in a flimsy little boat. Columba and his disciples had big-time decisions to make. They had to decide whether to leave the familiarity of their homes for a dangerous missionary voyage. Jesus' disciples had big-time decisions to make, and they would have even bigger ones after Jesus' death, resurrection, and ascension. No wonder Jesus assured them he had given them power to tread on snakes—to face their fears in order to make right decisions for ministry.

When the black bull snake crossed my path, I was in turmoil about a statement my bishop had asked all clergy to sign. If I did not sign, it seemed, the future of my ordained ministry in that diocese might be threatened. I tred on a black bull snake. I did not sign, and I am still doing ministry. When the winter-cold rattler shook her tail at me, I had some big family decisions to make. Argue? Accept quietly? Speak the truth in love or just love? That rattlesnake presented herself to be tread upon, and no family members are alienated as a result of the decisions I made. Four weeks ago, a small, slim, golden snake slithered in front of me on the path to the garage. I shivered and stood completely still. The snake climbed a

---

1. Butcher, John Beverly. *Telling the Untold Stories* (Harrisburg, Pa.: Trinity Press International, 2000), 70.

wall of rocks stacked around a tree, turned to look at me, and disappeared into a crevice.

Have you read D. H. Lawrence's poem "Snake"? Lawrence has an encounter with a gold snake one hot day by a well. Both, it seems, have come for a drink of water. Lawrence hears what he calls "the voice of my education" telling him to kill the snake. He writes, "But I must confess how I liked him . . . I felt so honored." The snake lazily crawls away and begins to enter a hole. Lawrence writes that a sort of horror overcomes him, and he picks up a clumsy log and throws it at the snake, who convulses out of sight. Says Lawrence, "And immediately I regretted it."

Like St. Columba, and Jesus' disciples, our lives and ministries will present us each with more decisions than we might care to think about. So, how will we tread on our snakes?

Author James Hollis writes that D. H. Lawrence's decision to throw the log was a shrinking before the largeness of life, a dissembling before the invitation to dialogue, a skittering away before the invitation to depth. In the end of the poem, Lawrence himself writes, "And so, I missed my chance with one of the lords of life."[2]

In the high desert where I live, and in your homes and your churches, snakes will slither across our paths. My prayer for you is that, like St. Columba, you will tread on your snakes with largeness of spirit, deeply, bravely, and wisely. Actually, I know you will, because Jesus has given that power to his disciples. Oh, yes, one more thing: in the Chinese calendar, 2001 is the year of the Golden Snake.

Rhonda Smith McIntire is Canon for Spiritual Formation at the Cathedral Church of St. John, Albuquerque, New Mexico.

2. James Hollis, *Creating a Life* (Toronto: Inner City Books, 2001), 78-79. For the complete text of the Lawrence poem, see James Reeves, ed., *Selected Poems of D. H. Lawrence* (Harleston, England: Heinemann Educational Books, Ltd., 1967).

EVENSONG

Scars of New Creation

2 Corinthians 5:17, 6:8-10; Luke 17:11-19
Matthew R. Lincoln

I WAS ONE of those lepers, and I wasn't the tenth—the one who returned praising God and giving thanks to Jesus for his healing. I was more like the other nine, who, as they went on their way and discovered that they were healed, said, "Hey, cool! Let's see if we can go back to our lives right where we left off when we got sick!"

My second child was born seven and a half weeks early. He and his mother nearly died. They both made it, and I was more grateful than words can describe. The birth was late on a Friday evening in Boston. A day and a half later I was back home on Cape Cod, working at church. I knew I needed to be there among the saints who were praying for my wife and my child. I needed to see them, be hugged by them—not just hear on the phone that they'd be praying for us in church. Still, I didn't miss that Sunday, and I didn't miss the next. After three weeks, I thought I needed to be in church again to show the congregation that the Lincolns were doing just fine, and everything was getting back to normal.

It came time to preach. I stepped over to the pulpit. For several months, I had been preaching without notes. Doing so required having an outline in my head so clear and so direct that each thing I said reminded me of what to say next until I reached my conclusion. (Not a bad discipline to develop, by the way. My listeners certainly appreciated it!)

So I launched into my sermon, and went along fine for about five minutes. Then my mind went blank. I stopped, apologized to the congregation, begged their patience, and tried to remember what I had been saying. When I couldn't even remember my last words, I tried to recall what the readings were, thinking I could say something simple and find a gracious way to stop as quickly as possible. Well, my mouth got so dry my tongue was sticking to the air, then my tongue got a little thick, and my words got fuzzy, then my peripheral vision got fuzzy. The next thing I saw was a halo of concerned faces: a nurse in the parish, the rector, and a couple of others, as they bent over me where I lay, quite comfortably, on the floor behind the pulpit. I wanted so much for life to be back to normal, and it wasn't.

I am fortunate to be able to say I have met two people who are more like that tenth leper who returned to give thanks. One of them is Lucy. I met her one summer at the Church of the Heavenly Rest, in New York City. I sat in the doorway, serving as a security guard disguised as a tour guide for visitors, and also doing what I could to help street people who came in.

Lucy came late one afternoon, seeking a bed in our homeless shelter and a refuge from the streets where she worked supporting her crack habit, and her pimp's habit as well. We were unable to take her in that night, but she wouldn't leave. She stayed nearby, and slept on a bench just outside the front door of the church, knowing that she needed to be hidden under the shadow of the church's wings. The next morning she was still there, so I called around and got her placed in a thirty-day detox program. She was so happy to think that she was escaping from her addiction.

Two weeks later, she was waiting at the front door of the church when I got there, crying and limping badly. She had left the program thinking she could make it on her own. She told me of the night just passed, of running from and fighting with her pimp all through Spanish Harlem and down to the river's edge in parts of town where nobody should go alone—not wanting any crack for herself, but forced to turn tricks to pay for her pimp's crack. She cried and cried, and through her tears, she raged, "When I left here two weeks ago, I thought this church was so good, and that God was taking care of me. Where was that God last night? There was no God with me last night!" She cried herself to sleep in a pew near where I was sitting. She slept there for three or four hours. When she awoke there was a beatific glow about her; her face was radiant. "You know what? I shouldn't have lived through last night," she said. "God must have been with me. There's no way I could have survived if God had not been protecting me every step of the way." And she continued speaking, praising God, and giving thanks.

I learned so much from her. Funny. Something like six years passed between the time I met Lucy and the time my son was born. During that time I must have forgotten some of what I had learned. I certainly felt grateful when he and his mother survived and recovered from the illness that required his early birth. But I didn't change how I saw myself, where I saw myself in the world. And I didn't change how I stood in the world accordingly. So I fainted in the pulpit from stress and exhaustion, when I thought my life was back to normal.

The other "tenth leper" I know is one of the saints of St. John's, where I now serve. Wally is in his eighties, and he passes his days in a round of quiet, unasked-for acts of kindness and helpfulness. He married late in life, and I think he feels lucky to have had so many years with Mabel, in spite of his late start. One of his routines is to put up the numbers on the hymn boards at church each week. One Friday night last summer, I went over to the church to check on a fan that I put into a window to draw cool night air into the building. (St. John's is in that part of the country still in denial about how very hot it gets in the summer, so there is no air conditioning.) Wally was there, putting up the hymn numbers. He said, "Ya know, we never had that fan in that window before you came . . ." He looked at me as if he had just caught me stomping through his favorite flowerbed. I said something like, "Yeah, I know. There just isn't much you can do with a new rector, is there?" He said, "Well, it's never been this cool in here, either."

Would you believe it took until last week, in my weekly prayer group—something like nine months—for me to realize that Wally was thanking me? It did! Now, you might say that Wally was not truly a leper, and you're right. But then, I'm not truly Jesus, either, so perhaps the illustration still holds together. And I think Wally's leprosy, such as it was, was not in his skin, but in his heart. And when he was healed, he was able to fall in love with Mabel, and marry her. And he loves her still.

But the leprosy has left its scars. Even though there is a new creation, the scars of the old creation are still there, so much so that it pained him visibly to thank me. And all I could see were the scars, so I missed the thanks completely. But now I know: Scars are sometimes signs of new creation. This is fascinating! And as I find myself among a group of people like you, people who know that God has changed their lives, I can't help thinking you may have some scars! I'd love to hear about them, about the new creation that they prove even as they obscure it! Perhaps, like St. Paul, some of you bear the scars of being treated like impostors, or perhaps of being ignored and unknown, or left for dead, or punished. Perhaps the small measure of detachment you have been given by grace has been seen by the old creation as sorrow, or poverty, having nothing. Are these actually signs of the freedom you have to be true and truthful, because you know you are known by God? Are they signs of some of the little deaths that made way for new life in Christ?

Sometimes it's so hard to know. One of the surest signs of new creation is joy right in the place of deepest sorrow. I saw that joy in my friend Lucy. After that day of sleeping in the pew, she got back into the program. That's unheard of, by the way; they don't give people second chances because it's a waste of resources. They were right, of course. She bombed out a second time. But a few days later, she turned up in a safe house in Spanish Harlem called "Hotline Cares." The guy who ran the placed called me on the phone and said, "Hey, Matt! You know some chick named Lucy? What am I supposed to do? I can't get rid of her! She's been cookin' and cleanin' around here for two days. Today I made her paint a room we painted last month, just to keep her busy. She says she won't leave here until we send her out of the city, because she won't be free until she gets away from the pimps and pushers who know her."

Well, we sent her to a detox program in Albany, New York. A month later, she called me from a pay phone on a street corner in Utica! She said, "It's so beautiful here. Did you know that when the wind blows, the leaves on the trees turn white?" She had never seen a silver maple before. "The houses here got grass growin' all the way around them! I been clean for more than a month! It's so beautiful here. And you know what? There is a man across the street. He is so handsome! And I have not even gone over to say 'hi' to him. I am not going that way any more."

Every breath she drew in, she breathed out with words of praise and thanksgiving. She looked poor, but she made me rich. She looked like she possessed nothing, but she truly possessed everything—except the thing that was the occasion of her call: "There's just one thing," she said. "I got no cigarettes. Can you send me some cigarettes?"

Matthew R. Lincoln is Rector of St. John's Church,
North Haven, Connecticut.

FEAST OF ST. BONIFACE

Taking Our Places at the Table

Acts 20:17-28
Anne K. Bartlett

I SUSPECT I am not the only one who plans imaginary dinner parties. If I'm dozing on the couch on a Sunday afternoon, or bored to tears at some interminable meeting, I'll occasionally amuse myself by figuring out the menu, flowers, list of guests. Ordinary constraints do not apply. You may invite anyone you wish, living or dead.

Today the honored guest is Boniface. Perhaps you do not know him well. I've asked around. My priest friend Bruce said the only thing he knew about St. Boniface is that "rich white guys name their churches after him." Mary, more recently ordained, mused: "Boniface . . . Whew. I *think* I know him. He lived back in those Middle Ages. He's an ident saint." "An *ident* saint?" "You know. If he shows up in a question on the General Ordination Exams you only need to know enough to identify him in a sentence or two. He's not an essay kind of saint."

Well, if I decide to keep Bruce and Mary on the guest list, they'd better clean up their acts. Besides Boniface, and me and you, the only other guest will be St. Paul, though he lived seven hundred years before Boniface was born—which doesn't matter in the least.

I don't know how to address St. Boniface. He was an archbishop, after all. But growing up in England when the Celtic influence was still so strong, his name was Wynfrith. That's what he was called at Exeter when he was a monk, and when he became a priest. His name was Wynfrith until he was middle aged and went to Rome. Pope Gregory II nicknamed him Boniface, Mr. "Good Works."

I'll keep the menu simple, so I won't fret like Martha in the kitchen. Good, crusty bread and olive oil for dipping, some cheese, olives in the bright blue dish, a savory lamb stew, a bottle (or two or three) of wine, and lots of water. That's enough. Fresh fruit—and chocolate—for dessert. I want to linger at the table.

Here's how I plan to introduce the two saints to each other: "St. Paul," I'll say, "Apostle to the Gentiles, meet Boniface, Apostle to the Germans."

And then I'll tell them how much they have in common: they both were missionaries, both wrote letters that we still read, both planted churches far from home, both respected women's gifts for ministry and used them in positions of church leadership. On and on I'll prattle until one of them stops me.

"We know each other well; we're hardly strangers. Paul taught me how to do the job, through his letters, though his witness, by his passion. He was my mentor and my inspiration," St. Boniface will explain. "Paul taught me how to stay the course, how to keep the faith when one is burdened with disappointment and frustration."

In Christ's Body there are no strangers. Which is why, of course, this imaginary dinner party I'm planning for St. Boniface seems so plausible, so possible. Church history is holographic, just like Scripture. Enter into it from any angle, and we all are there, in Christ. When we preachers homilize on Saints' Days, we slightly shift our famous three-legged stool to put tradition front and center, though the weight is still equally supported by Scripture and by reason.

The saints are human documents; their lives, sacred texts. In them (as in Scripture) we can learn to listen for the Living Word, alive and startling. The Word is embedded in their humanness, shining through their flesh. In our saints, we find Christ. That's the point. That's the joy. We're all in this together, in the Body of our Lord.

At our dinner party, I hope Boniface opens up his heart and tells his story, especially what made him, in his middle age, leave the monastery and go on mission into a foreign land. He was forty-three, for heaven's sake, no spring chicken. By all accounts, Boniface was greatly liked, immensely popular at home in England. His brother monks even chose him to be their abbot. But he chose to change his life radically and leave. "Ha! What makes you think he had a choice?" says Paul. Well, Paul ought to know about a thing like that.

It did not go well, Boniface's first foray into the mission field. The pagans were militantly hostile. ("You bet," says Paul.) I find my voice and tell them that at least the pagans in my world are not militantly hostile, though they do outnumber us in Oregon by four to one. They kill us by indifference. The heathens, and the pagans, and all the ones who say, "I'm spiritual but not religious," dismiss us Christians with quite a bit of condescension. This post-Christian world of ours has some striking similarities to pre-Christian ones. ("You got that right," agree Boniface and Paul.)

After failing at his first attempt, Boniface regrouped. Went to Rome. Received Pope Gregory's official blessing on his mission, began his years and years of unremitting work in the German heartland. Boniface strikes me as such a strange eighth-century amalgam of Celt and Roman, bureaucrat and missionary, shrewd politician and impassioned preacher, an integrated head and heart. Early on, he got dramatic, and one day in an extraordinary gesture chopped down the sacred oak tree that was steeped in pagan superstition, just to prove those old gods couldn't save. That's an act I won't follow. It wouldn't work, not where I come from.

But mostly Boniface preached the Gospel. At the same time he was saving souls one by one, Boniface organized and reformed the Church, built ecclesial infrastructure, did his best to clean up the clergy (their behavior was a mess). He constantly recruited his Christians friends from England. He talked men and women, priests and monks and nuns, to join him in the German venture. They established monasteries in the forests, churches in the towns, helped him bring order out of chaos, creating community in Christ's name.

Years passed. Boniface was made a bishop, then archbishop. He called councils that further tightened up the structure of the Church, gave it form. As a spiritual leader with some power, Boniface anointed kings and also articulated the parameters of Christian doctrine, for beliefs had gotten fuzzy and mixed in with all kinds of woo-woo spiritualities. ("Uh huh," says Paul. "Um hum," I add.)

Is there nothing new under the sun? This Christian life of ours, round and round we go, through centuries, millennia, but still the same old, same old issues? Well, why not? In each new era, the Church unfolds in fractal pattern, cruciform in shape. Each generation is to be conformed to Christ and live lives as the Church in the world of its own time.

So here we are, we modern missionaries, like Paul, like Boniface, told to go and preach the Gospel to all nations (even to our own), told to tell the Story to those who do not know it, to those who maybe once had heard it but who have long since forgotten or confused it, or dismissed it. Our age is as dark as any that has gone before; let's not be naïve.

"And don't kid yourselves about how hard it is," warn both Boniface and Paul. From history's perspective, their missions look like great successes, gracefully unfurling from their hearts and hands, the Light of Christ spreading like a glorious stain across the map, illumining the landscape. "That's illusion," warns St. Paul. "The only certain thing is trials and tribulations, sufferings, afflictions, and the bitter taste of betrayals by those you love At the least your hearts will break. And more than once. That's a given."

The conversation now deepens, darkens. Boniface quotes from a letter he once wrote to a woman friend back home, an English abbess to whom he had poured out his truth: "On every hand is struggle and grief, fighting without and fear within. Worst of all, the treachery of false [brothers and sisters] surpasses the malice of unbelieving pagans."[1]

At the table, the candles sputter. On the saints' faces, one can still see the traces of their tears.

"I am terrified when I think of all this," wrote Boniface, long before he died, before his blood was shed one day by local thugs in Frisia, while he was waiting by the river for some confirmands. (Out of the corner of my eye, I see Paul nod in deep understanding.) Boniface continues, quoting from another letter in which he had confessed, "I would gladly give up the task of guiding the Church which I have accepted if I could find such an action warranted by the example of the fathers or by Holy Scripture." The giving-up action is not warranted. Once bound by the Spirit to our task, we are committed.

Boniface has become our pastor and our priest today, at this party in his honor. He pulls no punches. Neither he nor Paul would have us be surprised by what we're getting into, by that commission to which we have agreed, which is to preach forgiveness in the name of Christ, our Crucified and Risen Lord, just as he bids us do. Paul says: "Here's what I believe, what I told the elders from the church at Ephesus that day. I said 'I do not account my life of any value nor as precious to myself, if only I may accomplish my course and the ministry which I received from the Lord Jesus, to testify to the gospel of the grace of God.'"

We ask the saints: "Tell us how to keep the faith, how to keep our courage, how to preach the kingdom?" Brother Boniface tells us—these are his words: "Trust. Trust in the One who has placed this burden upon us. What we ourselves cannot bear let us bear with the help of Christ. Let us be neither dogs that do not bark nor silent onlookers nor paid servants who run away before the wolf. Instead let us be careful shepherds watching over Christ's flock. Let us preach the whole of God's plan to the powerful and to the humble, to rich and to poor, to persons of every rank and age, as far as God gives us the strength, in season and out of season."[1]

---

1. Ephraim Emerton, ed., *The Letters of St. Boniface* (New York: Columbia University Press, 2000), 100.

Now in my reverie, I clear the table, put the dishes in the sink, blow out the candles. The party's over. No, that's not right. The party has begun, again, one more time, and will never end until the Kingdom comes. Boniface and Paul and you and I and all the others in that great cloud of witnesses come together 'round this table, where Christ Jesus is our host, and we the honored guests. Bound by the Spirit, may we now take our places there in fear and trembling, in sure and certain hope, and offer thanks to God for this life of grace to which we have been called.

Anne K. Bartlett is Rector of Trinity Church,
Ashland, Oregon.